In Season

UNIVERSITY PRESS OF FLORIDA

Florida A&M University, Tallahassee
Florida Atlantic University, Boca Raton
Florida Gulf Coast University, Ft. Myers
Florida International University, Miami
Florida State University, Tallahassee
New College of Florida, Sarasota
University of Central Florida, Orlando
University of Florida, Gainesville
University of North Florida, Jacksonville
University of South Florida, Tampa
University of West Florida, Pensacola

In Season

Stories of Discovery, Loss, Home, and Places In Between

Edited by Jim Ross

UNIVERSITY PRESS OF FLORIDA

Gainesville / Tallahassee / Tampa / Boca Raton

Pensacola / Orlando / Miami / Jacksonville / Ft. Myers / Sarasota

This book may be available in an electronic edition.

23 22 21 20 19 18   6 5 4 3 2 1

Library of Congress Control Number: 2017957524
ISBN: 978-0-8130-5695-1

The University Press of Florida is the scholarly publishing agency for the State University System of Florida, comprising Florida A&M University, Florida Atlantic University, Florida Gulf Coast University, Florida International University, Florida State University, New College of Florida, University of Central Florida, University of Florida, University of North Florida, University of South Florida, and University of West Florida.

University Press of Florida
15 Northwest 15th Street
Gainesville, FL 32611-2079
http://upress.ufl.edu

For Melanie, James, Anna, and Kate

Contents

Introduction

Jim Ross

Florida is a land of seekers. People come here for fortune, love, respite, entertainment, natural beauty. They long for a fresh start, or at least a recharged battery, and Florida promises to deliver. Witness the Disney commercials on TV or the online advertisements from residential retirement communities. It's great down here! Just get yourself on a plane or point your car south on the interstate. The Sunshine State will take care of the rest.

The essays in this collection slip beneath the surface of those promises and examine the reality. What do seekers find once they cross the Florida line? It's usually something they didn't expect.

These essays provide a Florida take on universal themes: the urge to leave home and start anew, the struggle to build a life in a different place, the clarity that the natural world can provide. The personal experiences differ, of course, but they point to this truth: The places where we live, or visit, inevitably put their stamp on us. "A place become us and we become that place," as essayist Susannah Rodríguez Drissi puts it.

When readers encounter a collection of Florida essays they might expect a bazaar of the bizarre. You may have seen "Florida Man" on Twitter and marveled at the weird crime that happens here. You likely have laughed at the work of Dave Barry and Carl Hiaasen. And it's true: Florida's zany politicians, miscreants, and wildlife often defy belief. I have written many crazy Florida tales during a 28-year newspaper career here. In the early 1990s I wrote about a man who showed up for his Citrus County court hearing wearing a T-shirt that depicted bikini-clad women standing in the bed of a pickup truck. Underneath the picture was the caption "Haulin' Ass." The judge, not amused, found the man guilty of contempt of court and sentenced him to 10 days in jail. Years later, racy T-shirt man ran for Congress. This being Florida, the only surprise was that he lost.

This collection features different kinds of stories. These essays, all but two previously published in literary journals and magazines, examine the quiet, private, personal moments that play out in the Sunshine State. No hanging chads or pages ripped from a *Miami Vice* script. Taken together, they help us better understand a state that is so diverse and full of contradictions that it defies easy classification.

Florida is a paradise in the marketing materials, but also a dangerous place to live, as Corey Ginsberg discovered as she fought to make her home in a crime-pocked neighborhood. It's a natural wonder, but also imperiled, as Lucy Bryan saw firsthand when she joined a student group on an environmental service trip in Apalachicola. It's a haven to immigrants but can't satisfy all of their yearnings, as Drissi realized when she arrived in Miami.

"Something constantly threatens to be out of control here," Lisa Roney writes in her essay. All Florida residents, and a good many visitors, know exactly what she means.

Yet despite its dangers, Florida also is a place of unexpected riches. Watch Sarah Fazeli come to Disney as a young woman to work as a character and receive life-changing advice from Merlin (yes, really). For Lauren Groff, a transplant from the Northeast, the life and work of Marjorie Kinnan Rawlings provide a welcome guide to her new home. "Marjorie found a way to let Florida bloom into something magnificent inside of her. I am still struggling to do so," Groff writes in one of two brilliant essays republished in these pages.

This collection features essays from two kinds of authors. Most, like me, grew up elsewhere (the Chicago suburbs, in my case), came to Florida as adults to live or visit, and then wrote about their experiences. Some pieces are from authors who were born in Florida or grew up here, left, then returned as adults to live or visit.

Many of us have struggled to understand what we found when we arrived (or returned) here. Reading these essays from my fellow transplants and travelers makes me feel less alone on the journey. The essays also remind me how much my adopted home state has shaped me. I hope you enjoy these very real stories about life in this very real, and very special, state.

The Lost Yearling

An American Classic Fades Away

Lauren Groff

Harper's, 2014

One night last April, I walked from my house in Gainesville, Florida, to the Matheson Museum, a shy brick building hidden by a thicket of palmettos and so small that the forty or so people seated inside seemed to make the walls bulge. I'd come for one of the first events in "The Year of *The Yearling*," the seventy-fifth-anniversary celebration of Marjorie Kinnan Rawlings's 1938 novel. Someone had made molasses cookies from a recipe in Marjorie's cookbook, *Cross Creek Cookery*, which powered us through a slide show: the backwoods Florida crackers who inspired *The Yearling*, the map of the scrub annotated in Marjorie's hand, the writer in sundry poses.

A woman as stout and dark as Marjorie stood before us in a boxy 1940s skirt suit, with a felt hat cocked to the side. This was Betty Jean Steinshouer, a scholar and Chautauqua performer steeped in Marjorie lore. She pulled out a flask and channeled the saucy, blasphemous, drunken writer for more than half an hour. A discussion of Marjorie walling up her barrels of moonshine to keep them away from her maid begot a more general consideration of Marjorie's dipsomania, which begot the story of her meeting with Ernest Hemingway in Bimini, which begot a meditation on Wallace Stevens, who came to dinner at Marjorie's and offended her so much that she jotted on his thank-you note:

From Wallace Stevens who spent an evening at Cross Creek being dis-
agreeable and obstreperous. Got drunk, read his poems with deliberate
stupidity. Held out his arms to me and said, "Come, my Love."

The others at the Matheson gobbled all this up, save one white-bearded
man who was snoring. During the question-and-answer session, a woman
with cropped silver hair stood and spoke mistily and at length about her
first time reading *The Yearling*, and a man apostrophized the taxidermied
bear in the corner of the room, calling him Slewfoot, the name of the canny
black bear that is the family's nemesis in the book. Then we were released,
and I made the walk home in the dark, our neighborhood hoot-owl flap-
ping from oak to oak beside me. I found I was terribly sad.

The Yearling was awarded the Pulitzer Prize. It was the best-selling novel
of 1938, and it has sold millions of copies since. The book remains familiar
in a vague way to many American adults, who probably read it in school or
have seen the 1946 film based on it. But it is more than a bestseller, and
certainly more than a dated children's book. It is a genuine classic, influ-
enced by Hemingway's declarative simplicity and edited by Hemingway's
legendary editor, Maxwell Perkins. For a time, its author was a literary
figure to rival the rest of Perkins's stable, which included F. Scott Fitzgerald
and Thomas Wolfe. Marjorie Kinnan Rawlings was friends with Zora Neale
Hurston, Martha Gellhorn, and Robert Frost. She corresponded with John
Steinbeck, Thornton Wilder, and Eleanor Roosevelt. She was Margaret
Mitchell's guest at the Atlanta premiere of *Gone with the Wind*. Her house
in Cross Creek, about twenty miles from Gainesville, is a state park.

And here's what "The Year of *The Yearling*" will have given us by the time
it wraps up in March: presentations on pets and pet care and the plants
and seasons in the book, tastings of cracker foods, a number of walks and
runs (such as the 5K Yearling Run and Scamper at M. K. Rawlings Elementary School), and various static exhibitions. There is little to entice people
not already fond of the book, and even less serious discussion of its literary merits. It seems as if the organizers, though they planned with great
goodwill, forgot to pitch the novel to anyone outside their circle.

At the Matheson, we'd been throwing confetti and dancing the schot-
tische, all the while ignoring the water lapping at our ankles. Despite the
torchbearers and the molasses-mouthed fans, *The Yearling* is slowly sinking into obscurity. The novel sold about 6,000 copies in all formats in 2012,

which represents a typical week for *The Great Gatsby*, *To Kill a Mockingbird*, or *The Catcher in the Rye*, if we count only the most popular of the many published editions of these books. When I asked Scribner what they were doing to celebrate the anniversary, I was told there was an illustrated edition being published in the fall by Atheneum, the house's children's division.

The Yearling is a magnificent, transparent, slow-moving river. Its style is direct and free of fireworks, its subjects planted at the beginnings of the sentences, solid as potatoes. The first chapter opens:

A column of smoke rose thin and straight from the cabin chimney. The smoke was blue where it left the red of the clay. It trailed into the blue of the April sky and was no longer blue but gray. The boy Jody watched it, speculating.

Like so it runs, for about 400 pages.

The cast is small, mainly keeping to a family of three crackers in the Florida scrub in the early 1870s.[1] They are Ezra "Penny" Baxter, a diminutive and gentle-hearted man; his wife, Ora, who has given birth to so many babies who died that she has almost no tenderness left in her; and their surviving son, Jody, who is between childhood and adulthood. Jody is dreamy and lonely. He has two friends: his father, and an addlepated, crippled boy nicknamed Fodder-wing. The Baxters live in the Big Scrub, a sandy triangle of land between the St. Johns River to the east, Gainesville to the northwest, and Ocala to the west. The Big Scrub is now the Ocala National Forest: there is a Yearling Trail one can hike, and the feel of the place is that of lurking danger and almost shocking beauty. There are sinkholes and springs and long swaths of spiny, lush foliage. *The Yearling* expresses both danger and beauty: the Baxters are surviving on the brink, one dead sow or ruined corn crop from starvation, but there are also glorious passages about the land, and hunting scenes that can get even my vegetarian-pacifist blood all het up.

---

1   A note on the term "cracker": though it seems pejorative, it is simply what the backcountry white settlers who came from Georgia or Alabama called themselves. Nobody knows how the name arose—perhaps as a bastardization of "Quaker," or as a reference to the bullwhips they cracked when herding cattle or the corn they cracked to make cereal, or from some name the Seminoles bestowed on them (which probably was, come to think of it, pejorative.)

The plot arrives a third of the way into the book, when Penny is bitten by a rattlesnake and almost dies. Struggling, in pain, he shoots a doe that has just fawned in order to draw the venom out of his arm and into the liver he cuts out of her. Penny survives, and Jody returns to rescue the half-starved fawn. Lonely as Jody is, he persuades his parents to make a pet of it and names it Flag. The deer becomes a playful, loyal makeshift brother to the boy. But when Flag becomes a yearling, his wildness kicks in and he endangers the family. Poor Jody is ordered to kill Flag. In one of the most heartrending scenes in American literature, Jody does, but then he runs away in fury and almost starves to death. He returns home unutterably diminished, but finally a man. As with so many great books, a summary of *The Yearling* makes it seem a bit silly. The novel's power is subtle, accumulating with every description of the natural world, until the book's rhythms become almost transcendental.

It seems odd that a novel so sensitive to Florida's natural environment was written by a carpetbagging Yankee, at least until you remember that most people who live in Florida were not born there. Marjorie Kinnan Rawlings didn't visit Florida until she was thirty-one, a married woman, and a largely unsuccessful writer. She had been a journalist for the Louisville, Kentucky, *Courier-Journal* and the Rochester, New York, *Times-Union*, where she wrote Songs of the Housewife, a daily syndicated verse series. Marjorie's poems are, I'm afraid, sheer doggerel. Some of them end in exclamation points, and they bear titles such as "Nose News," "The Jolly Tramp," "Other Women's Babies," "Itching for a Spanking." There is also the pie cycle: "Good Pie," "A Very Useful Pie," "Lemon Pie," "Cherry Pie," and the alarming "Ancestral Pies." The first stanza of the first poem she published, on May 24, 1926, goes:

> I call them twice to breakfast—
> Then, if they are not there,
> I let the smell of sausage
> Waft up the kitchen stair.

In March 1928, Marjorie and her first husband, Charles, visited Florida for the first time. She was gobsmacked by the beauty of the state, and late that summer, they bought an orange grove in Cross Creek, thinking that citrus cultivation would give them enough income and leisure to write. By

November, they had seventy-four acres with more than 3,000 bearing citrus trees, an eight-room farmhouse, a barn, a tenant house, 200 chickens, two mules, and a Ford truck. Cross Creek was the northernmost frontier of citrus cultivation, and the Rawlingses wouldn't have been able to keep the trees alive had the farm not sat on the narrow peninsula between Lakes Orange and Lochloosa, which softened the climate. Farming was terrifically hard work, especially at the beginning, and the Rawlingses had to battle freezes and droughts and malaria and the Mediterranean fruit fly, a pest so frightening and pervasive that for a while it seemed the state's entire agricultural industry would collapse from it. This was pre-DDT and pre-AC. Still, Marjorie loved the place. In *Cross Creek*, her 1942 essay collection, she writes, of the grove and old farmhouse, "after long years of spiritual homelessness, of nostalgia, here is that mystic loveliness of childhood again. Here is home. An old thread, long tangled, comes straight again."

She also found herself falling in love with the people around her. Her first notable literary effort, "Cracker Chidlings," is what one would fear from a Northerner who'd come south to write—a condescending piece of essayese based on what she saw of the illiterate, hookwormy people around her. But the next few years saw some of her most sympathetic and accomplished work: her two best short stories, "Jacob's Ladder" and "Gal Young 'Un," the latter of which won the 1933 O. Henry Award, and her 1933 novel *South Moon Under*, a brilliant and strange vision of contemporary cracker culture.

In November 1933, Marjorie and Charles divorced. She stayed on the farm with a succession of hands and maids to help. Also in 1933, Maxwell Perkins first planted the seed of *The Yearling* in Marjorie's brain, writing:

> I was simply going to suggest that you do a book about a child in the scrub, which would be designed for what we have to call younger readers. . . . If you wrote about a child's life, either a girl or a boy, or both, it would certainly be a fine publication, and such books have a way of outdoing even the most successful novels in the long run, though they do not sell many in a given season except now and then.

This was three years before Marjorie began to write *The Yearling*, and at the time she was still struggling to finish her (terrible) second novel, *Golden Apples*. She thought, perhaps reasonably, that writing for children would prevent her from being taken seriously. Eventually she concluded that *The Yearling* would "not be a story for boys, though some of them might enjoy it. It will be a story about a boy—a brief and tragic idyll of boyhood." With this in mind, Marjorie went bear hunting out in the backcountry with a friend named Barney Dillard and stayed with another friend, Cal Long, in the Big Scrub. She sent Perkins the completed draft on December 2, 1937, and he published it an astonishingly swift four months later, in April 1938.

Massive bestseller, Pulitzer, huge movie deal, Book-of-the-Month Club (the Oprah's Book Club of the era), on and on. After her years of disappointment, Marjorie was at last hefted to the stars. Except she wasn't. The struggle continued. She almost died from diverticulitis, an inflammation of the colon, and the disease dogged her for the rest of her life. She developed alcoholism. She abandoned the plans for her next novel, based on the life of Zephaniah Kingsley, an early nineteenth-century Florida planter. She wrote *When the Whippoorwill*, a story collection, which is good but not great. She wrote *Cross Creek*, which some people have tried to persuade me is great but isn't, fatally marred as it is by racism. She became distracted by love and married Norton Baskin, who owned the Castle Warden hotel in St. Augustine, where a Ripley's Believe It or Not! museum stands today. With the help of her maid, Idella Parker, she produced *Cross Creek Cookery*, which offers standard 1940s fare (Egg Croquettes, Lobster Thermidor, Tomato Aspic and Artichoke, Baba au Rhum) mixed with some eccentric Florida dishes (Minorcan Gopher Stew, Coot Surprise, Swamp Cabbage, Chayotes au Gratin, Loquat Preserves). She became involved in the 1946 film adaptation of *The Yearling*, starring Gregory Peck and Jane Wyman. A former friend, Zelma Cason, sued her for libel over this description in *Cross Creek*:

> Zelma is an ageless spinster resembling an angry and efficient canary. She manages her orange grove and as much of the village and county as needs management or will submit to it. I cannot decide whether she should have been a man or a mother.

The lawsuit soured Marjorie. She bought houses in Crescent Beach, just south of St. Augustine, and Van Hornesville, in upstate New York. Max Perkins died in 1947, breaking her heart; her heart suffered more literal damage in February 1952, when she had a coronary-artery spasm. In 1953, her fourth novel, *The Sojourner*, which she had labored over for ten years, was published to a critical whisper. She died on December 14, 1953, of a cerebral hemorrhage, and was buried in Antioch Cemetery, near her home in Cross Creek. Norton had discovered it was the wrong cemetery at the last minute, but Marjorie was buried there anyway, because he didn't want to bother folks by shifting her to the right place. If photographs from the Sun City newspaper are any indication, there were many flowers but few mourners.

These past few months, I haven't been able to stop wondering what happened to Marjorie and *The Yearling*. How does a classic run out of steam?

The first person I asked that question was my father-in-law, Clayton, who was born in Gainesville. He was once a boy like Jody, growing up in an alien Florida without air-conditioning or theme parks, and he may be one of the few living people who remembers meeting Marjorie Kinnan Rawlings in person. Clayton was a trial of a child, and to keep him safe in public places his mother put him in a dog harness. Par for the course at Disney World these days, but back then it was horrifying. This was about 1947; Clayton would have been five or so. He and his mother were at the Piggly Wiggly downtown. She'd forgotten the harness, and he was raising sheer hell. Suddenly a vast and angry woman loomed over him, bellowing at his mother, "Can't you control that child?" Clayton's parents owned a bookstore; his mother knew that this was the famous writer from Cross Creek, and she was mortified.

I took Clayton to lunch at The Yearling, a restaurant half a mile down the road from Marjorie's house, where a man named Willie Green played the blues and our server had never read a word of Marjorie's work. I'd heard the best thing on the menu was the venison.

Clayton and I have a rocky relationship, partially because I blame him indirectly for giving my husband the family business and thereby making me live in Florida, partially because he doesn't relish my personality. He is also now mostly deaf, and my voice is pitched where it is hardest for him to hear. He answered my question by leaning forward and talking earnestly about how nobody in Florida reads books, and when he was growing up nobody read *The Yearling*, it just wasn't important to the culture. He, who as a kid read a book and a half a week, never read it until he was an adult. It's not surprising that a book about Florida won't be read by people who don't read books, and the book is so profoundly about Florida that if people in Florida don't read it, who else is going to?

People in Florida *do* read, but I think he touched on something important: there is an internalized scorn of Florida shared by natives like Clayton and people from other states. Why read about Florida? What is Florida? As my neighbor Jack Davis—a history professor at the University of Florida—puts it, Florida is a "fantasy state and schizophrenic, not knowing whether it's Northern or Southern so it's nothing . . . It just doesn't fit in the national narrative, not as any kind of indelible regional state, so it can't sustain a book written in a Southern setting. People visit Florida or they relocate to Florida, but it is never home; Ohio or Illinois remains home."

Florida is the state where grown women impersonate mermaids for a living, where a family of egomaniacs is trying to build the nation's largest private home (they're calling it Versailles). Florida is where an armed adult can stand his ground before an unarmed teenager. Because nobody can understand what is happening in this state, Florida has become the butt of a million jokes. Even its shape is suspect: Florida, the dong of America.

Because she concentrated her work in Florida, Marjorie is seen as a regionalist. In this country, literary tastemaking begins in New York City, and regionalists can appear diminished by sticking to one place that is perceived to be less important. Marjorie is unlucky in that her finest work is Florida-based. Florence Turcotte, the archivist in charge of the Rawlings papers at the University of Florida, told me she believes that Marjorie would have broken out of her regionalist reputation had she lived longer. I'm not convinced: Marjorie's attempts at depicting other places weren't that good. Something about Florida sparked her alive.

Another factor in the fading of *The Yearling* may be Marjorie herself. She was not sexy. Though her stamp prettifies her, elongating her neck until it hilariously echoes that of the fawn in the background, she was matronly and angry-looking in life. She was not part of a school or a group—there was no Bloomsbury in Cross Creek—and at a time when Virginia Woolf and James Joyce were publishing their work, Marjorie was a writer of homespun people and straightforward realism. She did not have a spectacular death by suicide, just a brokenhearted, alcoholic one.

She had no advanced politics: she wasn't a communist, a feminist, or in the avant-garde. The most progressive thing she did was allow Zora Neale Hurston to stay in her main house rather than the maid's quarters. Of all the Southern states subjected to Reconstruction, Florida experienced the most racial violence. A black man was at greater risk of being lynched there than in Mississippi or Alabama. These were tensions Marjorie ignored in her work, even if she couldn't in her daily life. The word "nigger" appears several times in *The Yearling*—and not counterbalanced, as in *The Adventures of Huckleberry Finn*, by any overarching social commentary. Gary Mormino, a professor emeritus of history at USF St. Petersburg, says he nominated the book for the Tampa library system's "One Book, One Community" program, but that it was shot down because of its use of the word.

It also doesn't help that *The Yearling* is Marjorie's only first-class book. *South Moon Under*, her début novel, is full of intelligence and empathy, but its scope is small: it makes no swaggering claims. One classic book, two good ones, two terrible ones (not including the posthumous ones, which probably shouldn't have been published): this is a small, savory mouthful for a scholar hoping to dine on a subject for a whole career.

Worst of all, practically everyone I spoke to noted that *The Yearling* is considered a book for young readers. It is therefore shunted into a category beneath the regard of serious adults. It hadn't initially occurred to me that this could be a factor, primarily because I first read it as an adult and it was given the Pulitzer, which is not an award for children's books. I suppose some consider it to be a young-adult book because it's a bildungsroman drawn in sharp primary colors, written in accessible language, and bearing only faint traces of sex or humor.

I talked to Carolyn Harrell, a teacher at P. K. Yonge Developmental Research School, in Gainesville. She has been teaching for forty-eight years, which I found impossible because she looks barely sixty, with soft white hair and an unlined face. The kids who get Harrell are lucky: she speaks with such tremendous energy that she'd make chalk seem thrilling. Harrell is a Gainesville native and, like my father-in-law, didn't read *The Yearling* until she was an adult. She teaches it in phases over sixth, seventh, and eighth grades, supplementing readings with a visit to Marjorie's house, a hike through Ocala National Forest, and a feast based on *Cross Creek Cookery*. In all her years of teaching in Gainesville, so close to the place and history described in the book, she has never come across another teacher who has taught *The Yearling*.

She told me too that her students often have difficulty with the book. It is long, which is off-putting. There's so much description. The plot is slow. Children are reading less, and the statewide curriculum is going in the direction of short and dry pieces. Without Harrell there to push them, most of her students wouldn't read it. When her students do read on their own, they read fantasy, books about vampires and werewolves and other supernatural creatures. The average child who picked up *The Yearling* when it was released, during the Great Depression, would have heard the book speaking directly to him, in his world not unlike Jody's, with hunger and poverty all around. There may be hunger in the lives of potential young readers now, but it is different: few children would know what to do with a gun if a bear charged at them out of the dark woods, let alone how to feed their families in the wilderness.

Finally, *The Yearling* reflects a world we're losing, and does so in an orgy of carnage. Among the things killed and (mostly) eaten in the book are alligators, rabbits, deer, raccoons, squirrels, gopher tortoises (threatened), bass, bream, turkeys, foxes, possums, rattlesnakes, black bears (threatened), lynxes (endangered), panthers (endangered), curlews (endangered), and the last great wolf pack east of the Mississippi (critically endangered). Marjorie wrote of one of the final American frontiers, where nature hadn't yet been swallowed by civilization, but she came at it with sympathy for the killers, the people who slaughter the beasts in order to survive, and these days that feels wrong-sided. Steven Noll, another UF historian, told me that the history of Florida is a battle against water up until 1970, with dredging and drying up the Everglades and handling mosquitoes and humidity; since then, the battle has been to keep the water we have. By 1990, Florida had wiped out 46 percent of its wetlands, and the flora and fauna of the state suffered catastrophically. The aquifer is diminishing at an alarming rate, though the politicians in Tallahassee don't seem to be noticing. The more we pump, the more brittle the limestone layer between the aquifer and the surface becomes, leading to more sinkholes. The more we deplete the freshwater aquifer, the more the salt water of the ocean will intrude, hastened by rising sea levels. Once polluted by salt water, freshwater deposits are gone forever. The state of Florida will no longer be able to support its agriculture, its tourism economy, or its population of 19.3 million.

At The Yearling restaurant, my father-in-law spoke of climate change, but in personal terms. When he was a boy, the wildlife was far denser, he said. He collected snakes in his backyard; he saw raccoons and possums every day. He sees such animals rarely now. In the summer, there were daily microstorms that would blow through and cool the world off in a burst of rain. These, too, are gone.

"So *The Yearling* is, to you, a picture of a lost Florida," I said.

"A lost Florida," Clayton said. And this dry former statistician, whom I'd never seen show much emotion at weddings or births of grandchildren, put a hand to his mouth and cried.

Here's where I declare my own allegiance: I love Marjorie. I love Marjorie because of *The Yearling*, but also because our places coincide, and place is at the root of everything I've ever written. During my first difficult years of being a settler in Florida, I turned to *The Yearling* in hopes that it would teach me how to love this messy state. Like most people who read the book as an adult, I was expecting a children's book, and so was stunned to awe by *The Yearling*'s beauty and strength and by Marjorie's empathy for her poor and struggling characters. Later, when I looked into Marjorie's life, the coincidences felt uncanny: I've also lived in Louisville and in Madison, Wisconsin, and my husband's family has a place on Crescent Beach. Van Hornesville, where Marjorie owned her last house, is fifteen miles from Cooperstown, where I was born and raised; my mother taught biology at Van Hornesville's high school. But Marjorie found a way to let Florida bloom into something magnificent inside of her. I am still struggling to do so.

It is hard to be a person in love with *The Yearling* and the stunning landscape it evokes and not mourn their simultaneous passing. It feels inevitable that *The Yearling* will continue to lose its audience, that the state will continue to lose its native wildlife, that other species will continue to invade. The last time I went out to Marjorie Kinnan Rawlings's house in Cross Creek, Orange Lake was almost entirely dried up, and the little water I saw was covered in hyacinths. On the way there, we passed a smashed armadillo on the side of the road and our hood was stippled in lovebugs, swarms of insects that fly around twice a year coupled at the genitals. An introduced insect called the Asian citrus psyllid, which causes citrus greening (also called huanglongbing), is rapidly killing off the state's crops. Armadillos and lovebugs are both invasive species that Marjorie would have been bewildered to see.

If there's solace here, it's in the knowledge that not all change is to be regretted. A Gainesville-area boy was bitten by a rattlesnake in May, but these days we have ambulances and doctors who are not hopeless drunks.

Unlike Penny, the boy didn't have to kill a postpartum doe: eighty vials of antivenin later, he walked out of the hospital with the makings of a brand-new diamondback wallet. Every spring, thousands of new Flags are born; with the predators of Florida pretty much wiped out, the deer population is almost unmanageably large. Perhaps after Florida's aquifer is salinated and the state is rendered mostly unlivable, those who choose to remain will be the kind of gun-loving, off-grid survivalists to whom *The Yearling's* own gun-loving, off-grid survivalists will speak loudly and beautifully.

It is also true that only a lucky writer can write a classic, and it's only a rare classic that can be perennially relevant. If a book we love doesn't survive, it is maybe not the fault of the reader or the author or the book, but just that the world began spinning at a different speed than the book could keep up with. Someone is now writing the next blazing work that will inflame us all and then quietly and surely burn itself out. How glorious it will be for the short time it is alight, how much some lonely, struggling soul will need it. How bearable it will make living in the world.

The Same Creatures That You Fear

Lisa Roney

Numero Cinq, 2012

Birds

I live in the sky. Though it is crisscrossed with wires and impeded by bill-boards that sell big-breasted waitresses at the Wing House, it still dips its bruises in gold, not brass, then blushes at its own riches before waving good night. As I drive from yet another late neurology appointment along one of many six-lane roads that traverse the city, I search above it all, let the fading light guide me home.

Beyond the billboards, the barbequed chicken wings give way to the wings of hawks, eagles, herons, egrets. This evening eight ibis circle stunningly white against the blue, blue sky over the roadway, catching the last light of the day. Last week two bald eagles swooped ten feet above my head as I strolled my neighborhood. Cardinals and titmice flutter around the feeder in front of the kitchen window at morning and dusk, while the barred owls show themselves after midnight in their hilarious song. My husband and I lie in bed sometimes and mimic their "whoo, whoo, hah, whoo-who-oo-ahhh." It helps my insomnia when my heart is lightened this way at bedtime.

The anhingas even bring sky to the ground, as they sit lakeside with their wings outspread to dry, as if flying on earth. The birds are my favorite thing about Florida.

Winter Park

The first summer it rained and rained. In between the thunderstorms, I waited for my new job to begin and went on rambling, hours-long, solitary walks in the chic neighborhood near my homely concrete-block rental. One morning as I typed at my computer, I glanced to the right out the front window and faced a four-foot-long snake wending its way through the bromeliads under the orange tree.

At the time I didn't know the name of bromeliads. I said to myself, "It's only a black snake. Cool." But it might have been an omen of the unpredictable. I find later on that it is indeed adaptive here to enjoy the same creatures that you fear since you can't get away from them.

Medicine

Orlando is home to two of the ten largest hospitals in the country, and one of the three Mayo Clinic sites sits on the coast an hour north in Jacksonville. This does not assure anyone's good health—probably CEOs chose our locale for the aging (and dying) population of retirees that Florida is famous for. I myself came here young and immediately hit the wall of numerous health problems, as though crossing the border into the land of retirement infected me with oldness.

I came here with thirty years of Type 1 diabetes under my belt already, but my list of ailments has blossomed like a bougainvillea, taken flight like an enormous eagle: carpal tunnel syndrome, adhesive capsulitis, irritable bowel syndrome, rosacea, arthritis of the right foot, lumbago (only one letter different from the purple-blooming plumbago that I had never seen before coming here). The human body is part of nature, though certainly denatured by all the machines now engaged in being sick. In the past two years, I have endured a benign perimescenphalic subarachnoid brain hemorrhage and, supposedly in a completely unrelated set of incidents, inflammation of my brain pathways that may indicate MS. After six months of testing, they don't really know.

Even though I don't really want to talk about them, I cannot separate these things from what it is like to live here. The uncertainty seeps out of my skin like the constant sweat of summer.

Everywhere you go in Florida, there is a stark contrast between young and old—the stooped and graying alongside the tanned and buff, the slowest drivers in the world alongside the Daytona 500, the shops for orthopedic shoes alongside the surfin' bikini boutiques.

For most of us, living in Orlando is like living somewhere in between.

Heat

Our summer is our winter. Not that summer's cold, as in the northern-southern hemisphere switch, but in that we, too, have a season where we stay indoors, protected from brutal weather by our air-conditioning. According to the National Weather Service, more people die from heat than from any other weather-related phenomenon, including floods, lightning, tornadoes, and hurricanes. More than three times as many die of heat than cold.

One of the big differences between people who visit here and people who live here is that we are aware of the nastiness of the heat. Everyone stays outside a lot in December, January, and February. But we hide in June, July, and August, and we sweat profusely nine months out of the year.

Earlier this afternoon, as I walked into the doctor's office, a woman made a face and said, "I fear the spring is over." We bask in spring but dread the oppression of summer and fall, the threat of hurricane season.

Everyone in Florida carries a bottle of water. I first came to realize the Floridian devotion to hydration when I noticed that my students would sometimes get up during classes to go out and use the restroom. That is as accepted here as students blowing their noses in class in the North.

In fact, most of the people who die of heat exposure do so in milder climates where so many of the elderly still believe they can live without air-conditioning. Down here, we know we can't. If this makes me wonder why it is that people insist on living in such inhospitable places, I put it out of my mind. If I wonder, as I idle in traffic on my way home from the doctor's office, why humans have designed their world to be such an ugly and hostile place, I remind myself that the black lady standing at the bus stop on Route 434 with her umbrella up against the sun probably doesn't have the luxury to worry about it and neither do I, really, not these days.

Winter Springs

Six years after coming here, I got married and moved to the suburbs, not necessarily in that order. Both of these facts surprise me, and I feel guilty for liking everything about the suburbs but the political tenor and the car-time. Besides, everyone in Orlando drives a lot, no matter where they live. When *Men's Health* magazine reported that Orlando is one of the angriest cities in the country because of the traffic, I just nodded.

My new husband cackled. A Canadian, he declares America barbaric. "In Canada," he often reminds me when we're together in traffic, "we understand the concept of merging for mutual benefit. Here everyone races to the front and tries to jam their way in." I assure him that the entire country is not like this, but I feel the shame of American greed.

My own backyard reeks of stereotyped paradise, yet I love it almost as though it were my very own forever home. I was broke for a long time. Now the fountain bubbles, the cats roll on a bricked lanai, tall palms and pines line the fence, and two Adirondack chairs sit by the pool. I swim almost daily, though I did not want a pool and I am a terrible swimmer.

"Why else would anyone live in Florida?" my husband asked when I protested. I am not sorry I acquiesced.

I like being married after 49 single years and hope I still have plenty of years to enjoy it. I find it freeing to be tied. Once I thought I came here for the job at the big school over the previous small one, the moderate-sized city over the small town. Once I thought I would seek perfection until I found it and that excitement would always be mine. What a delight that I was so wrong.

Plants

Because flowers bloom year round here, and because there are few cemeteries, it can be easy to forget that the life cycle ends in death. When I get home, I pull my car into the garage and stand in the driveway, breathing in the aroma of the confederate jasmine I planted along the fence last year. I check on the new herb garden that is spreading exponentially, the way things do here. Finally, I am growing things.

It took nearly three years for me to plant the gardenia that a friend brought to our wedding, and it now has buds nearing bloom. All the other gardenias on the street parade massive, fragrant flowers, but I am thrilled simply that ours is still alive, gardenia and marriage both surviving over-work and hospital stays. The staghorn fern that another friend brought as a wedding gift hangs from a tree in the front yard. On cold nights, the neighbors down the street wrap their huge staghorn in blankets, whereas ours is still small enough to drag in the front door. I wonder if the enor-mous one down the street testifies to a long marriage and whether ours will get that big.

I have also put into the ground three offsets from an agave that grew in my Winter Park yard. These are an exception to the ever-blooming of most tropical plants. They bloom only once—on a stalk that appears overnight as tall as a telephone pole—and then wither into a heavy stump.

Finally, after the agave amazed me with its theatrics, I started to learn the names of more common plants: saw palmetto, sago palm, bougain-villea, bromeliad, bald cypress, mangrove, ligustrum. We have plumbago, shrimp plants, lorapetalum, and camellias growing in our yard. Knowing the names is almost as important to me as growing them, but I am glad to have reduced the amount of evil St. Augustine grass by half. St. Augustine grass is another one of those peculiar Florida phenomena—a non-native plant ubiquitous for lawns, it tolerates the heat but soaks up ridiculous amounts of water.

The hummingbirds will come to our new fire bushes and spicy jatropha. My newlywed husband will be here tomorrow in spite of my surprise brain hemorrhage and the lesions that could render me crippled or dopey. I will still be able to walk around and deadhead the flowers for some time. That is enough, along with the jasmine, for today.

Whorelando

The corporate tagline for Orlando is "the city beautiful," but we have coined the moniker Whorelando, or, in a more Spanish spelling, Jorlandó.

Though it still asserts itself over and over, the beauty of Whorelando is for sale and disappearing fast. I have never seen more strip malls any-where. When I originally looked for a house to rent, I clicked excitedly on an online ad for a "historic" home, only to find that it was built in 1950. Whorelando is full of concrete block and bulldozers.

I moved here nine years ago and have lived here longer than nearly anywhere in my adult life, yet it still feels alien. Like the narrator of William Gass's short story "In the Heart of the Heart of the Country," I am not of the people, not of the place. Like that narrator, I've had my disappointments.

On one of my first drives to work here I watched a man, a bag of McDonald's on his handlebars, a case of Coke strapped behind his seat, cycling alongside the traffic, his long, grey hippie's beard and locks flowing in the warm breeze, his pale face grizzled with dirt. Weird is everywhere I look. Sometimes it is the weird that is ultranormal—the made-up housewives with pink sweat suits and boob jobs, the nurse that says my survival is a gift from God, the sleepy kids lining up for the school bus.

I am in the heart of the heart of the heart of the peninsula, land-locked in a state full of beaches. We should get out to the coast more often.

Disney

Friends and family fly in and stay with us while they visit the "attractions." Everyone thinks that if you live in Orlando, you live close to Disney, so they are always surprised that we live an hour's drive away.

I have not been to Disney World since 1972, although I have had Pluto in class, and my husband, Cinderella.

Sanford

A few weeks ago, Trayvon Martin was shot and killed on a street in the town just across Lake Jesup from where we live. Orlando boasts tourists from all over the world, but just over the lake, whichever lake, there is a dense scrub of raw lawlessness and backwoods sensibility. Trayvon Martin's death by vigilante is the tragic other side of Peter Matthiessen's *Killing Mr. Watson*, in which an Everglades community bands together to murder a greedy bully. Something constantly threatens to be out of control here— the crime, the law, the lawless order, the construction development, the real estate boom and the real estate crash, the bougainvillea vines, the wind, the rain, the heat, the humidity, the drought, the Cuban tree frogs, the alligators.

Lake Jesup is full of alligators, and sometimes during mating season they come down through the creeks and end up in the retention pond across the street from our house. An eight-foot one took up residence the week before we got married in the backyard. "That just makes it a Florida wedding," my vet's receptionist told me.

My friends warned me before I took this job—about the fundamentalist Christians who objected to any mention of Halloween, about the hurricanes, about the gators and the palmetto bugs, even about rampant entrepreneurialism, capitalism gone jungle-feral. Some of them have cut me off because I came here. Some others have kept in touch for the vacations. I understand both impulses.

Rainstorms

After I come in from breathing jasmine air, I find an e-mail informing me that my teaching schedule for next year is in disarray. I spend a moment furious, but it's the usual way of things in a state with a legislature intent on destroying educational institutions that have only ever had a toehold anyway. The governor just approved creation of a brand-new state technical university, with the budget coming out of those of existing schools. Rumor has it that the legislator who sponsored this new school stands to make a killing on nearby real estate. All that valueless swampland once sold to unwitting northerners is now valuable after all.

The next morning, clouds finally move in after more than a month with no rain. We've reveled in the sunshine, but the splatting drops on my morning walk break the tension. By afternoon, it will be pouring off and on, and the smell of ozone will waft in through the open sliding glass door as I sit at the computer. I will stay home cozy with my husband in the evening because going out during rain here means getting soaked. We will watch for the neighborhood red-shouldered hawk, who often comes down to the low branches in the rain.

A friend down in Tampa says that she hopes the rain will come their way, though she hopes she doesn't regret wishing for it once the rainy season socks itself in for the duration.

"Sunshine State" is another misnomer around here. It rains constantly most of the summer.

My first year, I ruined six pairs of shoes by getting caught in unexpected storms. Now I just take my shoes off and smile when I walk barefoot into class or a meeting. Bare-assed, barefoot—I've learned to live with both conditions in my professional life.

The second year I was here, three hurricanes marched through Orlando. "They never come this far inland," a Florida native friend had said. I lay in the hallway of my rental and listened all night as the huge live oaks thundered to the ground in pieces. I thought, *this is what the apocalypse will feel like.*

Winter Springs Redux

A neighbor told me that her family had installed a new security system for fear of home invasion. Later, after Trayvon, she mentioned that her mother warned her son not to wear a hoodie. I don't know how to feel about that. Orlando has one of the highest murder rates in the country, but violent crime is concentrated far from where we live, and I find suburban fear rather silly, a little racist. As a white teenager, our neighbor's son is in little danger. But I am glad that the grandmother sees the absurdity of Trayvon's death enough to feel the fear herself.

For me, the more salient neighborhood concern is the possibility that I might run over an animal. Though the plants seem to bloom forever, the area is strewn with roadkill. Squirrels feed in the right-of-way, jerking their tails and dashing, often right into the street, when I pass. When one is killed in the street in front of our house, I am glad that the bald eagle that flies in to rip it apart first pulls it into the yard across the street, where it will be safer from cars.

The residential hawk, grabbing an anole, swoops down and pulls out the neighbors' window screen. My husband tells them so they won't think it's a robbery attempt. Anoles dash across the sidewalks, but their squashed bodies are nearly as common as their flickering live ones.

The raccoons take to tearing the screen out of the lanai, pooping in the pool, letting the cats out. We catch a raccoon swinging from the squirrel-proof bird feeder, back and forth, unhooking it and dumping the contents. We humanely trap and relocate two and an opossum in three days, but more come back. We install a raccoon baffle on the bird feeder. We install super-strong screens. Then we glue them in.

The armadillos dig up the front grass looking for worms and grubs. When I drive home after dark, four or five cross the street in front of my car. I know they are ready to leap straight up into my bumper.

Maybe living in more urban areas allows other people to forget that they are supplanting so many other forms of life. Here in the suburbs, we can never forget. An uneasy cohabitation prevails. I love the critters, and perform the sign of the cross as I drive by their corpses, but we also battle them.

Over dinner after the clarifying rain, I admit to my husband that maybe Orlando is indeed the quintessential American place—teeming, insane, unstoppable. For better and for worse, I tell him and wink. Probably the future doesn't look too good, but I have seen amazing turnarounds happen in my own departure from spinsterhood and my survival of my brain ailments. I have some hope that, after all the people are gone, Florida, if it dies by flame and not by drowning, will rise from the ashes. It seems at least the most likely place for resurrection.

Encyclopedia Floridiana

Lia Skalkos

Contrary, 2012

Green Basilisk / *Basiliscus plumifrons* / Jesus lizard

My roommate Frank finds the basilisk on one of his worksites and brings it home. He puts it in the snake tank, which he leaves on the patio, and tucks some plants in it to make it homey. Sheena puts a towel over one side of the glass so the lizard has shade.

The lizard is a bright, acid green—the kind of green that could only be found in a reptile. It has a crest on top of its head that fans out when it is alert and deflates when it is at ease. Its face is intelligent, though also inanimate in a very un-humanlike way, and it has a long, thin tail—so long as to seem gratuitous. Frank holds it with one hand, its tail protruding pornographically from between his fingers. I wonder if its heart is pounding. If it is, the lizard shows no sign of it. All those years of evolution and it is holding still in a hand that could crush it. I wonder: How does the lizard know when to stay still and when to run? How does it negotiate the balance between coming and going? Between stasis and instinct?

"Come see this," Frank says, still clutching it.

We all go out to the cul-de-sac in front of the house. Frank kneels down on the cement, lowers his hands, and opens them. Then the lizard is a moving green flash, a blip in our vision. It is running by us upright, on its two hind legs, bipedal, as if it has been hiding this fact from us all along. The thighs of its two legs are comically out of proportion to the rest of its body. They churn the lower legs like crankshafts on propellers. The lizard looks like the Road Runner, its upper body strangely stiff, even as its legs whirl and it is a blur of light. Its sphinx-like expression remains even as it is making a run for it.

"Runs like that over water," Frank says, then fishes the lizard out from under the rim of a tire.

"No way," I say. But later, I look it up and find it's true. In videos Jesus lizards fly across the surfaces of streams, the thin webs between their talons preventing them from plunging in more than an inch at full speed.

Frank returns the lizard to the tank and it eats a worm, some grasshoppers, a hibiscus flower. I keep thinking about how different it is from mammals. One day, while Frank has it resting on his shoulder, it darts off and one of the cats claws it.

"Didn't think so much blood could come out of a lizard," Frank says. I go to see and the floor is indeed filled with small pools of red. I am startled. Somehow, I was not expecting red. In some part of my mind, I was expecting the lizard to bleed blue or green, like toxic waste, or futuristic battery acid. Somehow, I imagined that the lizard—with its scaled skin and speed and stoicism—was untouchable, god-like.

Florida Blue Jay / *Cyanocitta cristata semplei*

The twin blue jays (are they a couple?) make an appearance on the patio almost every morning. They are haughtier and more aristocratic-looking than their scruffy, conventional blackbird competitors. It is hard not to stare at the blue jays. They are all hard lines and beautiful geometry: the feathered ridge on the head like a mohawk, the shifting shades of cerulean against the snowy-white plumage, cordoned off by the necklace of black. The thick triangle of the beak a perfect contrast to the slope of the bird's head, to the horizontal ridge. And, of course, the eyes like two black beads.

Frank doesn't like them because they shit on the patio and because they can't be chased off easily. But I am mesmerized by them. How they are arrogant together, in their coupledom.

Lovebug / *Plecia nearctica*

On the drive down to Florida the air filled with the long bodies of black flies the size of almond slivers. They had red thoraxes, as though they were wearing tiny red capes, and kamikazed themselves into the front of the car as we drove down 95 South. Some of them, I noticed, were attached at the end. There was something about this that made me feel bad for them. How cruel to have to be glued together in order to mate. To be Siamese-twinned against a car going 65 miles an hour.

By the time we were outside of Orlando the grille of the car was positively slicked with lovebug paste. They covered the walkways and doors like black snow, and we couldn't help but scratch and slap ourselves, imagining that they were brushing up against our skin. We were told that they only come out a few weeks a year, and that they infested this part of the state because the University of Florida accidentally released them during a science experiment.

"It's true," a cashier at a gas station tells me. "I had a friend who was working in the lab at the time. He was there." He says this with a conspiratorial nod.

The lovebugs are Romeo and Juliet, brought together by fate, mated for one tragic night, and then obliterated until their next reincarnation. I have never experienced such in-the-blood necessity. I still try to feel out the boundaries of my commitments, like a person in the dark. If I press tenderly, how far will they give? Will they stretch all the way to Florida?

And not only this, but the corpses of *P. nearcita* become acidic after a day or so and begin to eat at the car paint. How strange, I think. Driving into Florida during a downpour of suicidal, paint-eating lovebugs. It makes me nervous, as though they were the plague God forgot to send down. As though they were a silent warning to my need for motion, the reason why I am here.

Giant Toad / *Bufo marinus*

Every now and then we see the toad on the patio. He (or she? I always assume, unfairly, that reptiles and amphibians are males) is like a temperamental lover, only calling when the leftover cat food is still out.

If the toad was a person, it would be thought of as ugly. It has fishlike, wide-set eyes and skin the color and texture of swamp mud. Its heavy mouth sags. With all that skin, and being as big as a dinner plate, it is also corpulent. Bulbous but compact. There is something sensual about the toad. All that rutted, muck-brown skin, the face that is all body. The cats mewl at it with longing, thwacking themselves into the patio door for it.

"I want to let the cats out, but I'm worried it's poisonous," Sheena says.

I research. According to the University of Florida's Wildlife Extension site, *Bufo marinus* secretes a milky-white toxin from its parotoid glands. The poison will burn eyes, make cats and dogs foam at the mouth, cause convulsions. "Good thing we didn't let the cats out," I tell Sheena.

It turns out that, like so many other species here, *B. marinus* isn't indigenous. They established themselves in south Florida, the article says, after "about 100" of them escaped from a dealer at the Miami airport in the 1950s. When I first read this, I thought the article meant not a hundred toads but a hundred *exotic animals* had escaped. I pictured a burst of zebras, elephants, and giraffes surging forth from a cage, the exodus from Noah's ark, ready to thrive in Florida's warmth, the helpless pet dealer watching from the side. And then I checked and realized no, it was just the toads. I had to remind myself that, though Florida is known for its invasive species, not everything is trying to come here. Not everything is always looking for a new beginning.

And then, as I read on, I find out that, suspiciously, the giant toads were released again in the 1960s, apparently to assist with pest control.

B. marinus looks almost exactly like its southern cousin, *Bufo terrestris*. The only way to know the difference is to check for ridges on the head and for the parotoid glands that angle over the shoulders. *B. marinus* is ridge-less and has little hillocks of poison above its arms.

Both *B. marinus* and I are transplants to Florida. Me, for the summer, *B. marinus* for good. I want to lift it up from the tiled patio by its underarms, to see its limbs hang down. I want to hug it, to feel its amphibian, too-big warmth on my chest and the ridged, abraded skin, slick and foreign against my neck. Both *B. marinus* and I have been embraced by this strange land, our beauty and ugliness both finding their uses.

Northern Curly-Tailed Lizard / *Leiocephalus carinatus*

The curly-tails are dune-colored, and when they bask in the sun they lean horizontally, as if their joints are stiff. Their tails raise and tense into a nautilus before they dart off. Whenever I am leaving or coming back to the house, they scatter through the bushes or across my line of sight. Anytime there is a bit of movement without clear cause, I know what's behind it.

Tropical Orbweaver Spider / *Eriophora ravilla*

Walking up the driveway one night, I feel the unmistakable silk of a spider's web tangle across my shoulder and I cry out in terror. Out of the corner of my eye, I see the spider's body glimmer in the dark, the color of moonlight. I run inside and find a flashlight. When I shine it, the orbweaver contracts inwards. Thin-legged and skull-bodied, it is the size of a lychee. Its web is a wonder, a tapestry of gossamer concentric rings. In the dark the web is barely visible, so that the spider looks suspended, unearthly. I text Sheena and Frank to watch out for it when they get home. Night after night, we return to the driveway to awe at it. Its exoskeleton is perfectly pieced together, like the parts of a jigsaw puzzle. Its legs hook gracefully, are bent like talons. Never will I recover from the surprises Florida has to offer. Never will it stop giving me something else to wonder at, as though, once I feel I know everything the world has to show, it will say *no, look, hear, see.*

Ball Python / *Python regius*

Frank's snakes live in the closet, coiled up among the button-downs and jeans. They are ball pythons.

"But what if they get hungry?" I want to know.

"They don't come out," Sheena tells me. They ingest a rat once a month. When they aren't in the closet they are in the tank, but the lizard lives there now, so the snakes occupy the closet full-time.

There is something unsettling about the snakes, though I like them and have probably suffered more at the hands of the cats than I will ever from them. Perhaps it is some remnant instinct that reminds me that they are capable of killing humans. And they are so different from legged creatures, which is what I am used to. I like the long arm of their body, all muscle, corseted by the paper-smooth gold and brown skin. The clench of them wrapped around a limb—like an arm, or a shoulder—is so much stronger than I could have predicted. A little neighbor girl comes over to see them and her mother requests that they be put on her lap, apparently to make her overcome her fear of them. They sit on the couch together and Frank drapes one of the snakes over their legs and then promptly wanders off, leaving me to deal with the girl's screams to take it away. I grasp the snake a few inches from its head, where my hand can encircle its circumference. I pull it toward me, but it's like trying to grip the current, or the tide. The snake seems to bend in dimensions I didn't know existed, nearly thwarting me, though I am pulling it toward me with all my strength. I am humbled by the power of its body. I now understand viscerally that the snake could strangle me if it wanted to, all coil and squeeze—the world's worst tie, necklace, choker.

American Alligator / *Alligator mississippiensis*

But I cannot write about Florida, cannot catalogue its fauna without writing about the alligator. I saw them in an Everglades park. A keeper gave a talk on them in their enclosure, where two of them were basking by a palm. Using a stick, the keeper prodded at them, making them flee into the murky brown pool nearby. From utter rock-stillness they became pure movement, pure slippage in the water. The keeper tucked the stick into the largest one's mouth so we could see how wide the jaws open. The keeper was, in my opinion, a little cavalier.

The horny exterior of the alligator and its stillness allude to the prehistoric. They seem to know something we don't. Perhaps, it's eat or be eaten. Or that time extends in unimaginable stretches. The studded belt of their tails looks like armor against all tragedies.

I associate the alligator with Florida's strangeness, which I find alluring and beautiful. Forget the beach, the turquoise waters, white sands, tropical fruit. Give me the swamps. Give me the alligators. In Florida, quirk is an aesthetic. Unlike the North, here disruption is desired, needed. Here, creatures as old as history lurk in water the color of soil, their eyes comically peeping out like the periscope of a submarine. Here, people get drunk and get mauled by them. Yes, give me Florida any day.

Banyan / *Ficus aurea* / Florida Strangler Fig

The multiveined banyan trees appear, rope-like, throughout the South, though they are not as common as the palms. Their trunks are webbed in by roots, so that they appear to be all root, and no trunk. They are the color of wet paper, a charcoal, ash-gray. I want to crawl into the nest of those roots, exposed, tender, and fall asleep.

I have fallen in love with the banyan trees, just as I have fallen in love with Florida. How to tell you of the things I saw? How they took care of me, in their own way? How to catalogue all the wonders of the world?

The Cone of Uncertainty

Katelyn Keating

Lunch Ticket, 2016

Monday, 3 October

St. Johns County has been placed in the 5 day forecast cone by the National Hurricane Center.[1]

At five in the afternoon, I finish a writing assignment and send it away over the ether. I collect *H is for Hawk* and a highlighter and walk to the housing development's private pool for some uninterrupted reading. The air outside feels perfect, dry and warm. Hurricane Matthew is still far from where I live in St. Augustine, Florida; still a day south of Haiti. Matthew is an abstraction.

In the parking area by the pool, my neighbor Jerry leans into the security guard's car window, talking with her.

He sees me, beckons me closer. "You might not want to go to the pool," he says. "A lady died."

The security guard adds that the pool is open again. "It's no longer a crime scene," she says. "If you want to swim."

Jerry says the security tape shows the lady was swimming laps alone, then she reclined in a chaise and messed with her phone. And then she stilled.

Wait, which chaise? I think.

I turn and walk back to the house. I can't process this beyond wonder-

---

1   St. Johns County EMS: Situation Report-1 Hurricane Matthew.

ing, fleetingly, what is wrong with me. *Which chaise*. I want to read *H is for Hawk* in my favorite chaise—not today anymore, but next week, after the sun comes out again. *Matthew will wash it all away.*

At home, I tell Chad, my husband. I use Jerry's lingo: "A lady died at the pool."

We live with my father and stepmother, Jane. We moved across the country last year with our five pets to their spacious Florida townhome to cohabit while I'm in graduate school. The arrangement is saving us thousands of dollars each month. I was able to quit my career to focus on my MFA. Life in my parents' gated community, with its Thursday landscaping racket, thrice-weekly curbside refuse pickups, board meetings, and proliferation of security cameras, is not a lifestyle I'd choose, yet it sustains me. It works for now because we've set a time limit, and because these aren't the parents who raised me. They were the fun parents to visit every third weekend. Even still, there is a gratitude/attitude continuum. I occasionally behave as though I'm in my teens, not my thirties. So after I tell Chad, I find my parents and try to shock them with the news: "A lady died at the pool." They are not startled.

In the late evening, I walk the dogs and run into Jerry in his driveway. I get three mosquito bites while he tells me what he's learned since we first spoke. The lady's husband found her at the pool. The emergency responders did CPR for twenty minutes. There was blood, inexplicably. The lady and her husband have been renting at my parents' complex while they build their dream home in a nearby development. Their house will be ready in two weeks.

I ask Jerry questions he doesn't know the answers to: How old was the lady, and do they have children? I keep other questions to myself: *Is the husband alone?*

Tuesday, 4 October

The County is expecting to experience at least Tropical Storm conditions . . . [2]

Waiting for a hurricane takes patience. I grew up in coastal Massachusetts. I've waited like this before: Gloria in 1985 and Bob in 1991. Two

---

2   St. Johns County EMS: Press Release-2 Hurricane Matthew.

months after Bob it was the No-Name Storm, later known as the Perfect Storm. A few hours before a rogue wave would swallow the fishermen of the *Andrea Gail*, we walked from our house to Fort Sewall. When the wind gusted just so, I leaned out over the bluffs marking the entrance to Marblehead Harbor, my stepfather's hand on my belt for precaution, and felt the wind lift me up, hold me aloft.

Today, I have an essay to write for the journal I work for. I don't take days off from my studies. But I can't concentrate; this hurricane is on my mind. Conditions need to be favorable for writing: chores done, desk clean, some quiet—Matthew is disruptive. He is destroying Haiti on my second monitor.

I waste my writing hours thinking about storms past.

Wednesday, 5 October

Morning: *A Hurricane Watch has been issued for St. Johns County.*[3]

The essay should go to my editor today. I'd normally be on my third draft by now. I don't miss deadlines. Instead, I have an opening paragraph and an idea that I liked until I sat down to write yesterday. Now again, I should write. Other things preoccupy me, like the husband of the lady at the pool, and Matthew, who destroyed Haiti yesterday and is now in Cuba, and the ice and water we still need and probably won't be able to procure by later today. Images of bare shelves cycle through the news updates.

I was going to write about my dad and me, and Bob Seger, how there's an inheritance in music. As a teenage Deadhead I scoffed at the pop end of the classic rock spectrum. My stepfather's vinyl collection showcased the psychedelic sounds I worshipped then, while Dad's music seemed square. But approaching forty now, a strange time to live with parents, I see a convergence. Like my dad, I now unapologetically and unironically love Bob Seger: the husky high baritone; the melodies; the lyrics about drifters and hot sultry nights. Maybe another time for this essay—Matthew consumes my words.

Afternoon: *St. Johns County has been placed under a Hurricane Warning.*[4]

---

3   St. Johns County EMS: Situation Report-3 Hurricane Matthew.
4   St. Johns County EMS: Flash Report-5 Hurricane Matthew.

We won't have enough dog food. No one has gone yet to get ice or water and it's probably too late, the stores stripped clean of necessities hours earlier. Chad loaded the truck with the pet supplies I packed in case we need to evacuate; he loaded the truck when I insisted. I'm certain our little teardrop RV over in storage will be a goner.

Chad has never waited for a hurricane. We've lived in evacuation zones for tsunamis, earthquakes, and avalanches, even in Tornado Alley. He is unperturbed, working remotely in his home office for a company in the Midwest. Dad and Jane have been through two hurricanes in this townhouse. They are unperturbed. Dad's watching movies.

I interrupt my work, again and again, to scribble lists of emergency items in case we need to evacuate, to refresh my browser for updates from the county, for updates about the rising death toll in Haiti. I wait for Matthew to bring danger.

I want to read *H is for Hawk*, or think about the husband of the lady at the pool. *What is he doing while waiting for Matthew? Is he planning a funeral?* Weather alerts ping, and I'm worrying about two friends who are out of town: Who is caring for their pets? And another friend who just became a mother: Will she cling to her baby on her roof on Friday? Instead of writing my essay I'm thinking about the thousands of Haitians who just lost everything. I watch roiling streets of water in Haiti on TV and remember the rising waters of Katrina.

I listen to Governor Rick Scott's press conference. I print the pets' rabies certificates and gather some valuables and study the county's pet-friendly shelter brochure. From an Instagram post, I learn that I don't have to go to work. The farm-to-table restaurant where I wait tables part-time is closing unexpectedly early for hurricane preparation.

It's unfathomable to some people that I gave up my career in a field I once loved, gave up my two-story 1906 Craftsman with hardwood floors and a fenced backyard, to return to the student life; that I work once more in restaurant service, like a young woman; that Chad went along with it. It's complicated—I couldn't not write any longer. And after fourteen years in motion for Chad's career, it was my turn. It's also simple—I'd rather be a thirty-nine-year-old server trying to be a writer than someone working in a cube not writing. In case one sunny day I go to the pool and never stand up from the chaise, I will have tried.

Thursday, 6 October

Hurricane Matthew is a dangerous category 4 hurricane with sustained winds of 140 MPH . . . [5]

At six this morning, two county zones went under mandatory evacuation orders. We do not live in an evacuation zone. The hospital is closing. The airport is closing. We are staying. I wonder about the husband of the lady at the pool: *Will he be alone and what will he eat?* The number of dead in Haiti rises.

Jane waited outside for the grocery to open this morning and bought ice. Chad procured the eighteen gallons of water I decided we needed— three gallons per day for each person, plus six more for the pets. The necessities were back in stock. Earlier, the absence of these items seemed predictive that we would suffer.

Things to do: make oatmeal to supplement the dog food since the replacement is delayed by Amazon; grind coffee; drive to the RV in storage to collect tarps and the coffee percolator; endlessly refresh the emergency pages on social media for the county alerts and the weather. Evacuation supplies need to be packed into a laundry basket, and the cars need to be repositioned with the truck in the driveway, ready to load pets and go. I have the husband of the lady from the pool and all the Haitians to think about.

Still no essay about me and Dad and Seger.

Friday, 7 October

St. Johns County is urging all residents to stay indoors and off the roads . . . [6]

Matthew will be here today. Before the inevitable power loss I run a load of laundry and take a shower. The water is cool because Dad and Jane and Chad each showered before me. Jane fills the home's only bathtub. The waiting that has consumed days is now collapsing into hours.

The NWS warns this will be the first major hurricane to impact our region directly in 118 years. There is no one with living memory of the last storm.

---

5   St. Johns County EMS: Situation Report-5 Hurricane Matthew.
6   St. Johns County EMS: Press Release—Stay Indoors.

Outside, the neighbors bustle. Everyone regrets not leaving voluntarily. With wind now gusting and the pressure inverting I also regret not having left. But it's too late. The highways are snarled.

The power flits on and off. My laptop is old and the battery doesn't work, so I power down and switch to mobile. I hunker in bed with the dogs, watching local news on TV, cutting in and out, tracking all the emergency sites on my tablet: NWS, St. Johns County EMS, Twitter. Chad did yoga and is working in his office. Dad watches one TV in the living room, Jane, another in their bedroom. We convene in the kitchen every few minutes to share updates. The updates gain urgency: storm surge breaches earlier than expected downtown and is destroying our city, the oldest city in the country; twenty people are trapped in a B&B; a homeless man in a wheelchair falls off the Vilano Bridge and is rescued. The water rises.

At home, ten crucial miles west of the ocean, the power flickers and the wind and rain rage. There is nowhere I can go to lean into the wind, no bluff where I can surrender to the power of the storm. The dogs refuse to go outside to pee. The pond spills over and streams beside the house. Chad works, and asks why I'm not working, or at least reading. I am watching. I am waiting.

I finally crack *H is for Hawk* because I feel accused of not working. I devour chapters and almost miss a press conference, distracted by Helen Macdonald breaking my heart: "It struck me then that perhaps the bareness and wrongness of the world was an illusion; that things might still be real, and right, and beautiful, even if I could not see them—that if I stood in the right place, and was lucky, this might somehow be revealed to me" (151).

As dusk settles, I see on TV that kayakers paddle through the flooded downtown streets. Our rain stops but our wind still gusts. We must walk the dogs before dark. The wind batters my body and I can't look up at the trees to see if they threaten to fall. I can only look down at my dog and my feet and choose each step. Back inside, while we try to dry the dogs, our power goes out. It's the cusp of darkness. I'm humming Seger's "Against the Wind."

I immediately yearn for *H is for Hawk*, but I shouldn't waste the flashlight batteries. Officials warned that power outages will last days. The storm is moving north. I think of everyone downtown, storm-surged, wet; now dark. I think of Haiti and the husband of the lady at the pool: *Is he alone?*

In less than an hour, power is restored. We start drinking and watch the original *Total Recall*.

Saturday, 8 October

Urban Search and Rescue operations are underway in affected areas.[7]

I sit in bed with coffee and read Lizette Alvarez's Thursday *NYT* piece about being trapped in a Category Five hurricane in South Florida: "But, like any good suspense story, the second half tumbled into terrifying." I'm thankful I didn't read this yesterday.

I walk the dogs. Every fallen stick looks like a snake. The sun shines and the wind feels warm and perfect. We'll go check the RV, see if it's a goner. The water recedes downtown and the National Guard might let people back in soon. I didn't start the essay about Dad and me and Bob Seger.

I want to finish *H is for Hawk*. It's a beautiful day for the pool.

Aftermath

St. Johns County residents are urged to stay vigilant.[8]

I watched Matthew on TV in bed with my dogs while he struck around me. Our town is ravaged, though no one died, no one was stranded on the roof. It was nothing like Haiti. Matthew was an abstraction and then he was wind and rain and downed limbs. He was storm surge. Then he moved on to Savannah and Charleston, and North Carolina to kill. The husband of the lady at the pool topped my list of worries, but has also dissipated to my east.

My fears came to pass, for others. Others suffer. I watch them on TV. Today, I'll help my friend haul everything she owns out to the curb. Her house stood with two feet of water inside for too long. Tomorrow, I'll help again, with my hands. I'll donate to Haiti with my heart, and my wallet.

---

7   St. Johns County EMS: Situation Report-9 Hurricane Matthew.
8   St. Johns County EMS: Situation Report-15 Post Hurricane Matthew.

I prepared for eventualities while a trip to the pool on a sunny day can be the end. Matthew changed the course of my writing for five days. I am still an adult living with her parents in Florida and working in a restaurant, striving to be a writer, to be a good grad student. Matthew left me unscathed.

How I Spent My Summer Internship

Jim Ross

Clockhouse Review, 2013

Every time I see a story about newspapers being doomed (such stories are published on the Internet every hour or so) I hope today's journalism students, training now for digital media, might still have the kind of summer I spent in 1987 as a reporting intern at the *St. Petersburg Times*' bureau in Pasco County. It was the best summer of my life.

As a sophomore at Northwestern University and a reporter for the school paper, I desperately wanted to line up a summer internship. I applied to almost every paper hiring. I had never heard of the *St. Petersburg Times*, and I didn't know a soul in Florida. Mike Foley, the *Times* recruiter who came to Evanston in the fall, said he wanted to interview only juniors and seniors. I signed up, anyway.

Tall, wiry, and long-haired, Foley wore thick glasses and a perpetual smile. He was like a grown-up version of Boon in *Animal House*: suave and cool and always ready with the right wisecrack. I confessed to breaking his "juniors and seniors only" rule. Foley loved it. He was a rebel, and he thought I was one, too. He hired only one intern from Northwestern: me.

The editors at the school paper, all older and more accomplished than me, were surprised. So was I. A rebel? I went to church every Sunday and worked at the library. I was a virgin and had never ingested any drug stronger than alcohol and aspirin. Think of Evan, the meek Michael Cera character in *Superbad*. Certainly, Foley had made a mistake. Later, an editor one rung down the food chain from Foley called my dorm room to talk summer arrangements. U2 blared in the background as I answered. No one important ever called my room. I scrambled to kill the volume. The editor, Joe Childs, thought this was hilarious. One editor thought I was a rebel, and the other thought I was a rocker. I figured when dork-o college boy hit town they would cry "false advertising" and demand a trade.

During spring break I flew alone to Florida to arrange summer housing. I stepped outside the Tampa airport and was assaulted by Florida's wet-blanket humidity. There was a palm tree outside the terminal door. A palm tree? I grew up in the Chicago suburbs. Our airports had asphalt, more asphalt, and then a different shade of asphalt outside their terminal doors.

I had paged through an AAA guidebook in search of "affordable" motels near downtown St. Petersburg. I was pleased to find one that allowed me to pay day by day with traveler's checks. I arrived to find an aging, red, single-story edifice with storm doors that opened into the parking lot. If my mom had been there she wouldn't have gotten out of the car. I couldn't have been happier.

I drove my rental car to see Foley at the first big-city newsroom I'd ever visited. He took me into his office and told me I actually wouldn't be working in the big headquarters; I'd be north of the city, in the Pasco bureau. I asked why. We need good people up there, he said soberly. *He needs good people up there!*

Go enjoy yourself tonight, Foley said. Drive west to St. Pete Beach until you get to the Don CeSar hotel, the huge pink palace, and turn left. Go to the Hurricane Lounge and have a fish sandwich. Then spend tomorrow holed up in your bare-bones motel room doubled over with food poisoning. Well, Foley hadn't mentioned that last part.

With one day lost to violent illness, I drove north to Pasco. I checked into a new motel and leased a studio apartment for the summer. What was the management company thinking? I was 19. Perhaps trying to validate Foley's image of me, I presented myself at a local bar (uh, I forgot my ID at home?), but the bouncers there, unlike the local landlords, took age seriously.

In June, on my first day of work, I wore a short-sleeved shirt that was too big and a tie that was too wide, both handed down from my dad. I shook hands with the bureau chief, Jeff Testerman, a sandy-haired, mustachioed man who reminded me of Burt Reynolds. Jeff had been a banker before he became a journalist, and his knowledge of public records (deeds, mortgages, land records) remains legendary at the *Times*. Pasco's intern the previous summer had been a house sitter for Jeff and his wife and had called them, alarmed, to report multiple lizard sightings outside their home. The reporters still laughed about that "discovery." What gaffes would the new boy make?

I was assigned to cover cops, and I went to the Sheriff's Office for the morning briefing with Bob Loeffler, the cheerful, portly public information officer. I returned to the newsroom all excited. Three people had stolen a 100-pound pig and roasted it. Theft! Arrests! Stop the presses!

I proudly relayed my find to Jan Glidewell, the paper's columnist in Pasco. Must have happened in West Pasco, he said. How did he know? If it had been East Pasco, he said, they would have raped the pig and then eaten it.

Glidewell had curly white hair down to his shoulders and a belly that invited comparisons to Santa Claus. Well, a Santa who is a nudist and a Buddhist. Glidewell once noticed that his desk was wet each morning. He learned the night cleaning lady was sprinkling holy water on it, hoping to ward off his evil spirits. He once wrote an entire column all in one sentence and referred to an I-75 rest stop as a "poo poo palace."

There's only one Glidewell, but the rest of the newsroom wasn't far behind in spirit. The guys (and it was largely a boys' club) joked all day and traded lines from *Stripes, Animal House*, and especially *Caddyshack*. They were talented young men trying to write their way out of the bureau and into the downtown newsroom. But the pressure was less intense in Pasco than downtown, so the place was like a small fraternity house, minus the beer.

We ordered Domino's on Friday nights and ate lunch together at Morrison's Cafeteria. Testerman held up a long stick with a tiny, plastic dinosaur head on the end. A trigger moved the mouth open and shut as he sang "Feelings." We had post-deadline scooter runs around the inside of the newsroom. I had the fastest time for two laps: the advantage of youth.

I never laughed that hard at my college newsroom, and I never felt so accepted, either. By then they all knew I was a dweeb, not a rebel, but I also was eager and prolific. I wasn't competing against anyone, like at the college paper. I wasn't competing against the other interns, all of whom worked in the big newsrooms in Tampa and St. Pete. I wasn't all stressed out trying to be a student and a journalist at the same time. I was just "the intern": part mascot, part journalist, part goofy younger brother.

"Send the intern!" was the favorite cry. When a sinkhole opened or someone robbed a bank, I shot out the door. I drove to a local community center that some teens had vandalized. They had spray-painted "Dead Milkmen" on the wall. John Cutter, the assistant city editor, was impressed I knew the band. Finally, some street cred.

During that summer, the *St. Pete Times–Tampa Tribune* turf war was surging into overdrive. Each paper had expanded its reach, crossing Tampa Bay and trying to steal market share. It became one of the nation's best newspaper wars in one of the nation's best newspaper states. It was a golden age in Florida journalism. The *Miami Herald* was breaking national stories. Tom French was at the *Times* and writing "A Cry in the Night," one of the classic works of literary journalism. Pasco County was part of the greatness, too. Just two years before I arrived, Lucy Morgan and Jack Reed had won a Pulitzer Prize for taking down the Pasco sheriff.

But none of that made much of an impression on me at the time. I was like a college basketball player who was allowed to play with the Celtics for three months. I didn't stare at the banners in the rafters; I just tried to score every now and then and make sure the man I was guarding didn't get to the hoop.

My competition on the cops beat was Dave Sommer, a deep-tanned, deep-voiced reporter with the *Tampa Tribune's* bureau in Pasco. Each morning Dave and I sat in Bob Loeffler's office and combed through reports from the previous night's arrests. We asked for copies of reports that looked interesting and had private talks with Bob, then or later on the phone, to pursue independent angles.

I wrote about drug busts, sex crimes, RV thefts. A man forcibly stole the engagement ring right off the finger of his very upset, and very pregnant, former fiancée. A truckload of frozen orange juice concentrate was stolen from a shipping company and set on fire. I conducted a jailhouse interview with a con man who had partied with TWA stewardesses who believed he was Jon Bon Jovi. I did the occasional news feature, including one about a bar whose two bouncers, Tiny 1 and Tiny 2, weighed almost 1,000 pounds combined.

My desk faced Charrie Hazard, the editorial writer, one of only two women in the newsroom. One day, some newsroom chatter turned to sex and someone asked me a question. "How should I know?" I asked with a red face. Charrie laughed gently. It's easy to forget how young you are, she said. If only she knew. I visited a veterinary clinic for a story and, a short time later, summoned the nerve to call back and talk to the beautiful receptionist. What would you say if I asked you out on a date? She laughed. I'd say my husband wouldn't want me to accept. The intern hadn't seen her wedding ring.

That was bad enough. But my naïveté almost got me in real trouble. Deputies arrested a man in connection with the murder of a convenience store owner. I went to interview his neighbors in Moon Lake, a rural area with unpaved roads, trashy mobile homes, and livestock wandering about. A seasoned reporter would have gotten in and out fast, and maybe brought a photographer along for safety. I wandered in alone and was gone for so long that Testerman sent a reporter to bring me, or my corpse, back to the newsroom.

I spent most of my free time alone, but there were a few memorable newsroom parties at staffers' homes. Late into one such soiree, a colleague impressed with my deep voice suggested I sing "The Lion Sleeps Tonight" and then join him in drinking a metal tub full of beer. I declined both invitations. At another we all downed tequila shots and watched *Caddyshack*.

On my last day, Childs and Testerman called me in for an exit interview. Did you break any laws this summer? They were joking, but unbeknownst to them the true list included DUI, careless driving, underage purchase of alcohol, and lying about my age to get into a bar. Maybe I was more of a wild man than I thought. Or maybe I had become one. Someone asked if I was happy the internship was over. No, I said. But I need to get back to college, where the party scene is tamer.

I didn't see Foley again until fall, when he returned to Northwestern for his next recruiting trip. He took me to dinner and we sat in an office at Fisk Hall, the home of the journalism school. There we were, two rebels, talking about the new round of applicants and trying to find the *Times'* next intern.

The Eternal Gulf

Rick Bragg

Southern Living, 2012

To pick one day on this water, one above all the rest, is like trying to hold on to the white sand with your scrunched-up toes as the receding waves pull it from beneath your feet. The Gulf occupies a shining place in our memories, of rushing, crashing blues and greens against a shore so white it hurts our eyes, of flashes of silver through shallows clear as branch water, of pink babies screaming with laughter as they outrun an inch-deep wave onto safe, dry sand, as if winning that race was the most important thing in their lives, till the next one. And when they are old it will still be that way, because waves are always waiting, one more summer, to race again.

I wondered if we would lose it all that spring and summer of 2010. Some old men, who know things like tides and the habits of fish, told me not to fret, that there was too much water out there to be killed by even such a gout of oil. Other old men, tears in their eyes, told me the Gulf only seemed eternal, that mankind could kill it like any other living thing. Now, two summers after, the crisis fades in our memories: The highways south are busier, the waits for a shrimp platter drag on a little more. And it is easy to believe again that it will always be there, a cradle for the fish, or just a place to ease our souls.

I will never forget the hopelessness of 2010, because little has been done to ensure it will not happen again. But it is not what I choose to remember.

I will remember a day when I was a young man in a small boat, drifting on the currents where the flats of Tampa Bay flow into the Gulf, water changing to a deeper blue, shadows of sharks in the shallows, me cursing at cormorants who snatch my bait as it hits the water. The captain, Joe Romeo, told me fish stories as rays glided like flying saucers across the bottom, till it was time to unwrap a Cuban sandwich and open a freezing can of Coke. I could stay, I remember thinking, stay and fish and tell stories and live on speckled trout and grits. But I would not. I would give in to ambition, and give this up. But before we quit that good day, I hooked something different, a glittering silver torpedo that, even now, remains one of the most beautiful things I have ever seen. "Lady Fish," Joe Romeo said matter-of-factly, as if some other fool had caught a fish this pretty and it had not made the newspaper. We let it go, but I never let go of it. I catch it, in my memory, over and over again.

Or maybe I will remember the day my mother, aunts, and little brother came to see me in Clearwater, bringing fried chicken cooked in an iron skillet and homegrown tomatoes and five plastic Purex jugs of water from Germania Springs, because everyone knows Florida water is not fit to drink. They got up the next day before dawn because they just do things like that, and we drove to a deserted beach. A pod of dolphins arced through the calm, flat water, and my mother hollered for me to get back because she believed them to be sharks and believes that to this day. When I told her they would not stroll ashore and get me even if they were sharks, she told me I might not ought to be so full of my little self. I watched my family drive away, waving from a butternut-colored Chevelle.

Or maybe I will not remember a day at all, but a night in Pensacola. After hours wide awake in a hotel bed, I dragged the bedclothes out on the balcony where the Gulf wind rattled the palm fronds and shifted the patio chairs. I made a bed from a comforter and a 99-cent air mattress, wrapped up in a giant beach towel, and let the rhythm and rush of that water, invisible in the dark, sing me to sleep.

The Crushing Weight
of a Giant Chipmunk Costume

Sarah Fazeli

Narratively, 2015

I was six. My family was at Disneyworld, making our way through Fantasy-land toward the carousel, when we heard a chorus of trumpets.

"Hear ye! Hear ye!" a voice boomed from a loudspeaker.

A man appeared, slightly crouched, in satiny purple robes, a long white beard draping practically to his legs. In a smaller, sweet and croaking voice, he spoke.

"Ahem," he cleared his throat. "Hear ye! Hear ye!" he shouted in a British accent, tr- tr- tripping over his words, his voice sliding up and down whole octaves. "By proclaim-, proclaim-, proclamation of King Arthur, I am here to find a temporary ruler of the realm!"

"Mom. Mom!" I yelled. "Stop! Everybody stop!" Through shouts and taps on shoulders and hand squeezes, the message was received by all four of my sisters.

"Sarah wants to stop here."

I moved slowly toward the front of the semi-circle of spectators and watched him, spellbound.

Merlin.

He revealed a wooden divining rod, and a mystical *"eeeeee"* tone sounded. He wrestled with the thick branch as it pulled him quickly back and forth, a start-and-stop sideways, stopping briefly in front of several people. He stumbled, unable in his old age to keep up with the fickle thing.

Finally, the divining rod stopped in front of a sturdy man, whom Merlin led to a silver sword buried firmly in a large stone. Merlin explained the importance of the word "Alakazam!" and instructed us to say it at the same moment the man put his hands to the sword.

There was a swell of music, a chorus of "Alakazam!" and . . . nothing.

The man could not budge the sword.

Merlin coughed and stammered, returning to his divining rod and scolding the branch for getting it wrong, this old thing. The temporary ruler of the realm had to be someone who truly believes in magic, he said.

"I do! I do!" I shouted, my arm flying up, my whole body bouncing, begging to be seen. I wanted to be the one pulled up onstage. I wanted everyone to cheer for me and see how special I was. "Please! Please!" I cried out, because I just knew I believed in magic more than anyone else did.

The divining rod drew toward me, Merlin tripped a bit, and I thought, "Yes!" But, the rod swerved and pointed to a little girl who was wearing a Cinderella nightgown as a dress.

He led us again in a chorus of "Alakazam!" and this time, with the child's hands on the top of the sword, it rose up with a triumphant flourish. Cheers and applause.

I was devastated. I did not get a chance to show everyone how special I was or how much magic I had inside of me. It wasn't fair. I believed. Tinker Bell, the Fairy Godmother, and Jesus had all taught me to believe.

Seventeen years after that Disney trip, it's my second year working at Disneyworld, and my first day in a new job at Ariel's Grotto.

I arrive at the Grotto, a watery pocket of Fantasyland where guests can meet Ariel from *The Little Mermaid*. Nearby, a bronzed statue of King Triton, water spurting from his trident, arises from a shallow green pool. There's spongy flooring and a small, wet play area with jumping fountains, a fancy version of playing in the sprinkler. Yellow and orange starfish punch up the gray-rock cavern. Seaweed dangles from a wide shell-shaped throne.

My job is to monitor guests' interaction with the red-haired mermaid, played by a glamorous girl wedged into sparkling aquamarine fins, her lips painted with coral lipstick and her large, possibly contact lens–enhanced blue eyes punctuated with feathery false eyelashes. This Ariel looks to be about nineteen, her petite hips settled firmly into her tail; long legs enveloped by luminescent scales.

Wearing my assigned wardrobe—boxy, mustard-yellow sailor pants and a formless beige peasant shirt—I watch Ariel reach out to embrace her admirers and feel a pulse of jealousy as adult eyes linger over her glossy purple-shelled breasts.

In college I played the comedienne sexpot Bianca/Lois in *Kiss Me Kate*. Wearing fishnets, I had sung the suggestive *Tom, Dick, and Harry* while dancing atop a large table, jumping off into the arms of three smitten, strapping suitors who carried me offstage, horizontally, their strong arms wrapped around my knees, thighs, and shoulders.

Here, I am not the talent. I am not pretty. I am not funny. And, I am not particularly trying to be. I don't know where that person has gone.

I feel slightly more important when I'm asked, due to a recent incident, to protect Ariel, vulnerable with her delicate scallops, from "accidental" brushes against her chest, and from furtive hands that casually molest her bare torso or the curve of her too-human body just beneath the thin fabric and sewn sequins.

The soggy lagoon smells of chlorine and pennies. There are two more hours until lunch, then three more until I can clock out. During slow times I focus on the coolness of the air, the sound of the waterfall. When it's busy, I take pictures for people and give advice on where to eat and which attractions to hit next. There is an influx of people after the parade. They line up to see this girl who gave away her voice.

I came to Disney aimlessly, after graduating from a liberal arts college where I studied music. My plans to pursue a creative career in Los Angeles or New York were foiled by a crippling onset of stage fright, and I moved back into my childhood bedroom for what became far too long. When a high school friend told me she was working at Disneyworld, I up and moved to Orlando. Maybe I could "make the magic" that I had loved so much as a child. That's what I told myself, anyway.

When I first started, I truly enjoyed dancing around dressed as a chipmunk; the gratifying, sweet smiles from kids and adults and the positive energy from the daylong hug-fests. But after six months in fur, the honeymoon was over. Maneuvering in the suffocating, heavy costume, breathing out of tiny holes in the big head, the Central Florida temperatures of ninety-six degrees were so hot and humid that the oblong plastic eyes constantly steamed up, sometimes to the point where I could see only blurs of faces. This put a damper on the drollery—and gave me chronic rashes and yeast infections. Dancing in the Spectromagic parade with a battery pack swinging back and forth along my sacrum gave me, like many others, chronic low back pain. I popped Advil like Tic Tacs.

"It's a *repetitive strain injury*," I would explain to non-characters, feeling somewhat like a fraud for using a term I associate with concert violinists and pro-tennis players.

But it wasn't the physical discomforts of the character job that wrecked me. Day after day, donning the woolly getup and bulbous head killed what little confidence I had left as an actor. I felt worthless and has-been at age twenty-two, working in this pseudo-performer job that anyone with half a personality and four limbs could do. For Christ's sake, I had done Lady Macbeth's "Unsex Me Here" speech, Noel Coward, Tennessee Williams. Was this how I was going to use my training . . . in a fleecy suit, with a hidden face? I knew I was playing small, squandering my youthful potential out of fear. Yet I couldn't seem to motivate myself out of the undiagnosed clinical depression and the immobilizing self-doubt.

One day, after wriggling myself into the Dale costume, adding an oversized green stocking cap and red scarf for the Magic Kingdom Christmas tree–lighting ceremony, I stood waiting for my cue. Mickey would look around for his gift for Pluto, and I would pretend I didn't know where it was. Minnie would wave her finger at me, and I would dig out a doggie-bone-shaped present, which I had supposedly socked away like an acorn, and would sheepishly hand it over. But when the moment came, the present was a little out of reach—I stretched awkwardly to retrieve it and felt something zing in my lower back.

A manager helped me hobble backstage. There was first aid, ice packs, then months of physical therapy, medical restrictions, and the first of several prescriptions for Vicodin I relied on just a little too much. This was the straw that broke the chipmunk's back: I needed to flee from fur.

I knew this, yet I couldn't seem to leave the Disney bubble. Where would I go? How would I pay rent? I would call long-distance from the pay phone in the tunnel under the Magic Kingdom, despondent, half in and half out of my shaggy body, and cry into the receiver to an old friend.

When a random job as an "escort" in Toontown opened up, I took it to save my low back. My trainer walked me into a small, cold room, uncharacteristically sparse in its decoration. There was only a large plastic Mickey-shaped pumpkin and a Goofy-shaped cactus in one corner, a blue ribbon painted on the wall where Mickey would stand.

My duties included motioning to small groups of people and ushering them to Mickey, where, in an orderly fashion, each party took a turn getting hugs, photos, and autographs from him in their shiny red autograph books.

"The most important part of your job isn't herding folks in or taking pictures," the trainer, a folksy but serious man, said. "It's to make sure this curtain is always pulled back so any stragglers from the other rooms don't catch a glimpse of another Mickey in the identical rooms. There is only one Mickey Mouse." Now this guy was really beginning to piss me off. I cleared my throat and clarified that I already knew all of this quite well because I was, after all, a former character.

"You left characters for Toontown Escort?" he asked. Now I was worried.

Within an hour of my first day as Toontown Escort, I realized I would be stuck in this isolating, windowless cell for nearly eight hours a day. For a place designed for photographs, the lighting was sallow and dim. If you were there for more than ten minutes, you would notice the dank, musty smell. The meet-n-greet room had all the charm of a construction trailer, and relied only on the live Mickey factor to bring it to life.

In the cooped-up confines of my Mickey room, wearing my red-and-white-checked uniform shirt, I would constantly look down at my Winnie the Pooh watch, the one with a bee as the second-hand. Time slowly ticked by. It was *Waiting for Godot*, Disney-style.

One day, a manager announced there would be a new post created, which we escorts would rotate in and out of. I was thrilled, rejoicing in the thought of escaping from this dreadful room, if only in twenty-minute increments. My enthusiasm deflated once I reached the assigned location: a small spot in a disorienting, winding green-carpeted hallway;

royal-blue-striped walls seemed to spiral to nauseating effect. Fluorescent-orange traffic cones flanked the doorway.

Guests were dumped through this exit in seven-minute increments, and they rushed out quickly, so aside from offering a few head nods and "have a good day" iterations, most of my time was spent wondering what I would die of first: boredom, claustrophobia, seizures brought on by loud colors and glaring optical illusion swirl patterns, or delirium from hearing the endless loop of the old-timey song "Turkey in the Straw."

I needed to get the hell out of Toontown.

That is how I ended up here, in Ariel's Grotto. A few hours into the job, I decide fresh air and the shaded cove area is, indeed, an improvement, but still feels pathetic. I took whatever quickie transfer I could to get out of the stifling Mickey room but quickly realized I should have pushed myself to something better instead of settling for just different. I leapfrogged my way across Disney that way—have I done that my whole life?

In the break room, the alternating Ariels, svelte girls all, are polite but dismissive of me, and make it clear they are interested only in reading their magazines and talking to each other. We are merely a few years apart in age, yet around these girls I feel youthless, the nurse to their Juliet, the ugly stepsister to their Cinderella. They are all skinnier than me, and I avoid eating my brown bag lunch near them. I try to keep my insecurities and shame silent, stifling my sobs in a break-room bathroom stall, and berate myself for giving in to this paralysis of depression and anxiety that is keeping me wasting away in Fantasyland.

Then, right there in the break room, I see him.

Merlin.

He is wearing his signature flowing royal-purple robes and is small in stature, even smaller because he's crouching forward reading a book. His small glasses rest so low on his nose they almost fall from his lined face. I would have thought they were part of his costume, but he appears to genuinely need them to read. He occasionally strokes his smooth artificial beard, and sips a cup of hot tea, all without ever taking his eyes off the page.

"Merlin." I say, star-struck. A girl of six again.

He looks up from his book.

"Well, hello there." He looks right into my eyes.

"Sarah, is it?"

How does he know my name? My face must reflect my astonishment because he motions with a skinny finger upward toward my shirt.

"Nametag."

Oh. Duh.

"Right. Yes," I say, blushing a bit.

"Cookie?" he extends a delicate one to me from a baker's-style parchment paper bag. I take it. We nibble together.

I ask what he's reading, but he wants to know about me. What are my favorite books? Plays? What do I like to do? Where have I traveled? Where do I want to go? Why had I come here? What are my dreams?

I tell him about my love affair with Shakespeare and obsession with *A Midsummer Night's Dream,* my dream of playing Titania, and my other dream role of Eliza Doolittle from *My Fair Lady*. I tell him I long to go back to London where I'd spent a few months interning at the Royal Court Theatre, about how the city captivated me—how the inspiration and lightness of the fantastical stories of *Peter Pan, Mary Poppins*, and A. A. Milne contrasted with the darkness of late medieval history and Dickensian times. The thoughts bubbled out of me fast and fervid, reminding me for the first time in a long time of the plans I used to have, the ones that extended beyond the gates of Disney.

Then he asks, matter-of-factly, when I am planning on getting back to performing again.

I sputter something about "eventually" and "I'll get back on track," but he persists. I deflect by laughing. "Anyway," I singsong, "*someone's* got to be here to make the magic!"

He ignores that. "Hmm . . ." he muses, lightly flicking his fingers together to brush away the crumbs. "Let's think." He closes his eyes and tilts his head back slightly. His chin juts out a bit. He looks as if he is concentrating deeply yet is also sound asleep.

"Ah!" his eyes flash open wide. "I have it. The festival. The festival!"

"What festival?"

"The Fringe Festival," he says. "Have you heard of it?"

I know what it is—a theater happening held every spring in Downtown

Orlando, featuring mostly original material with lots of solo shows and one-acts. I went to a couple of plays last year.

"You could do that."

"Do what?"

"The festival."

"Do what at the festival?"

"I don't know, dear," he takes a sip of his tea. "You'll think of something."

"Yeah, well . . . I'll think about it," I say, moving to get up. "Thanks."

He reaches out and sets a warm hand on my arm.

"What's there to think about?"

I blush. Merlin rises slowly, putting on his crooked cap and reaching for his divining rod. On his way toward the door he turns back, the divining rod pointing straight toward me.

"Creating something out of nothing . . . now that's making magic."

Merlin unruffles his vestments and floats out the door into the sunlight.

Dirty Hands

Lucy Bryan

The Fourth River, 2016

We've logged more than 15 hours on the road when we finally cross the Florida-Georgia line. The van stops on the shoulder of a two-lane highway, and we spill onto the berm—nine college students and me, the faculty "learning partner" on this environmental service trip. After stretching our backs and shaking out our legs, we snap a group selfie in front of a big, blue sign that says, "Welcome to FLORIDA: THE SUNSHINE STATE." A smaller sign with the words "Governor Rick Scott" hangs beneath it.

We haven't yet heard the news released this morning by the Florida Center for Investigative Reporting: Since 2011, Gov. Rick Scott has been subjecting state employees to an unwritten ban on the terms "global warming" and "climate change." At this point, though, we know little about the state politics that directly oppose the work we've signed up to do.

Truth be told, we don't know much about the place we're headed to—a nature preserve 50 miles west of Tallahassee. But the students know this: They live in a world that humans have polluted, exploited, and marred. And they want to help. They're propelled by youthful energy and an earnest desire to undo the damage our species has done. So instead of partying on white beaches an hour south of our destination, they've committed spring break to eating vegetarian meals, living on a poverty-line budget, turning off their cell phones, sleeping in tents, and planting wiregrass seeds for The Nature Conservancy.

As for me, I'm not convinced that we can repair what we've destroyed. And I'm skeptical of human meddling, even well-intentioned efforts to preserve what's left of our wild places. Although I look forward to learning about an endangered ecosystem, I seriously doubt that the work we do this week will have any meaningful environmental impact. In fact, I feel conflicted about our mission. Sure, we'll leave with a deeper appreciation of the complexity of our planet. But is that worth burning through more than 100 gallons of gasoline on a 1,600-mile road trip? Is it worth introducing bug spray, sunscreen, and micro-trash to the place we're trying to help? And might participating in a hands-on, management-heavy approach to conservation unintentionally make us complicit in the destruction we're seeking to remedy?

We drive into Apalachicola Bluffs and Ravines Preserve on a dirt road. My first impression of the place is that it looks disturbed. Spindly pines, cacti, oak shrubs, and tufts of dry grass jut out of an endless expanse of pale orange sand. I'm not sure whether this is a landscape of hardy survivors or foolhardy settlers, but it seems to be recovering from a terrible trauma. I am right, in a sense—though what I'm seeing is much closer to native habitat than what was here half a century ago.

We set up tents and hammocks in an oak grove near staff houses and a garage with a couple of open-air shower stalls built on back. Later, brown anoles scurry into the brush as we walk down the road to the preserve's education center. There, we cook a dinner of veggie fajitas and enjoy the sunset from a picnic table on the back patio.

The next morning, we return to the education center for an orientation led by Brian Pelc, a natural area restoration specialist for The Nature Conservancy. We learn that timber and paper companies clear-cut, windrowed, and established slash pine plantation on much of the preserve in the mid-20th century.

Long ago, before the arrival of European settlers, these sandhills were part of an open canopy of longleaf pine and native grasses that spanned the southern coastal plain. Maintained by periodic wildfires, Florida's longleaf savannahs became some of the most biologically rich regions in the temperate zone. Scientists have documented more than 40 plant species per square meter in the remnants of these communities, which historically provided habitat for gopher tortoises, red cockaded woodpeckers, and Florida panthers—all currently listed as endangered species.

But the fires that once would have swept across northern Florida at regular intervals—ignited by lightning or indigenous peoples—no longer burn. Fire suppression policies and man-made barriers, such as roads, have allowed hardwoods to dominate and transform the landscape. Less than 5 percent remains of the 90-million-acre longleaf savannah that once stretched from Virginia to Florida to Texas, nearly unbroken, according to The Nature Conservancy. The organization acquired the 6,295 acres that would become Apalachicola Bluffs and Ravines Preserve in 1982. Its work here over the last three decades is part of a large-scale, long-term project aimed at growing the longleaf pine ecosystem to 8 million acres by 2024.

During orientation, Pelc, who coordinated our visit, tells us The Nature Conservancy's goal is to "save the whole ecosystem." It's the kind of mission the students are eager to dedicate themselves to—the kind of mission that can fuel the monotonous and backbreaking work of planting wiregrass seeds for hours and days on end.

According to Pelc, saving the longleaf pine ecosystem isn't a matter of raising fences and letting nature take its course.

"You can't slap a lock on [the preserve] and walk away," he explains. "Property needs to be managed. What we figured out is that we needed fire."

We get a vivid representation of this principle when Pelc tows us through the preserve on a trailer. At one point, he stops and directs our attention to one side of the road—a restoration site that Conservancy staff burned about a year ago. We peer into a golden sea of wiregrass, interspersed with gently swaying longleaf pines. Then we survey the gray grass and crowded shrubs on the other side of the road, an area awaiting controlled burn.

It doesn't take an expert to identify the healthier ecological community. But I also see human interference everywhere I look. I see it in the skeletons of oversized oaks—selected for slow demise via chainsaw "girdling." I see it in the diesel-fueled tractors used to seed wiregrass into bare sand and the bright-blue tanks of biocide used to exterminate unwanted and nonnative species. I see it in invasive species themselves. When Pelc identifies a swath of cogon grass, cordoned off by pink flagging tape, I think: Who but the restorers could have introduced that menace so deep in the preserve? Surely it arrived in the grooves of a tire or the tread of a boot.

That evening, the students and I sit on oak stumps around the fire pit in our campsite and discuss what we've observed. This place doesn't con-

DIRTY HANDS · 57

form to our conceptions of wilderness. It's not uncontrolled, untouched, untrammeled. It's not, as wilderness historian Roderick Nash has put it, "a self-willed land."

"Maybe this isn't wilderness," I suggest. I point out that even if the native ecosystem is restored, it won't be self-sustaining. It will need humans because it needs fire.

This thought depresses me. If I had to hinge my survival on the unwavering dedication of a single species, I wouldn't pick humans. I'd probably go with some kind of ant.

At 8:00 a.m. Tuesday, we report to the on-site nursery. Its tables are lined with nearly 2,000 plastic seeding trays—each with 96 empty cells. Pelc explains that our goal is to plant as many wiregrass seeds as possible over the next three days. The plugs that grow in these cells will be planted by hand in areas that tractors can't reach.

Soon, we fall into a rhythm: Haul soil in a 5-gallon bucket and dump it over a tray. Tamp the soil into the cells with a wooden peg. Pour more soil over the tray. Tamp again. Place a pinch of wiregrass seeds into each cell. Spread a thin layer of soil over the seeds. Wipe the plastic borders between the cells. Repeat.

The simplicity of this cycle leaves my mind free to consider questions of scale. This week, our group will provide 240 hours of labor. If we plant 100,000 wiregrass seeds, and 75,000 of them germinate—that's enough to cover roughly 15 acres with one plant every square yard. That's just 0.2 percent of this preserve, which is a mere 0.08 percent of The Nature Conservancy's 2024 restoration goal (assuming all of the plants survive). It's hard to imagine this being enough, and it's easy to imagine it being too much.

Still, I enjoy the tactility of the work—the steaming soil mix, its coarseness and heft, and the wispy near-weightlessness of wiregrass seeds. Planting feels good, and a longing for it to *be* good rises within me. I want to be persuaded that our efforts (and the broader efforts they fall under) are helping this place.

That evening, we take a hike with a resident botanist. We walk down a dirt road and dip into one of the preserve's steephead ravines—extraordinary geological features that drew The Nature Conservancy to this site.

A network of underground rivers flows 150 feet beneath these sandhills, which were once the floor of an ancient ocean. And for several million years, springs seeping from the hidden waterways have carved deep, narrow gullies in the sand. During the last ice age, plant and animal species took refuge in the temperate forests this place provided. Many of them remained in the steephead ravines here after the glaciers retreated, creating a rare and remarkable ecosystem.

As we descend a sharp slope, the air grows cool and damp. We seem to have stumbled into an Appalachian Mountain hollow. Mountain laurel, beech trees, and white oak grow amid cypress trees and loblolly pines. We come to a clear stream at the base of the ravine and remove our shoes. For half an hour, we wade upstream alongside the salamanders and crawfish, and later we return to the banks to avoid a water moccasin. We also stop to examine the red blooms of a Florida anise tree and the delicate branches of a Florida yew. These "glacial stragglers" never returned north when the ice age ended and can only be found in this region.

The walk gives me the opportunity to talk to Damian Smith, a member of the preserve's restoration crew. I ask him why he thinks all this work—decades of human effort poured into this tiny speck of a place—matters.

"We're preserving natural history," he says, explaining that without such endeavors, this record of the past—and the rare species contained within it—might be lost forever.

I pose the same question to Brian Pelc the next day as we plant seeds together. He tells me that this project is doing more than creating a living exhibit; the preserve is also directly benefiting humans by creating clean air, clean water, and places to recreate. It may also have an important role to play as the effects of global climate change unfold, he says, since biodiverse habitats are better equipped than sparser ecosystems to handle losses and changes.

"But how do you weigh the benefits of intervention against unknown risks?" I ask. "How do you know there won't be some unintended and terrible consequence?"

Pelc's answer is practical: The team here uses a combination of expertise and instinct to make decisions—and they test interventions on a small scale before applying them broadly. The strategies that now enable the preserve's crew to restore 200 acres of ground cover per year have been honed and proven over time.

We put wiregrass planting on hold when a load of 700 longleaf pine plugs arrives—overflow from a nearby state park. The plugs need to get in the ground quickly, so we encircle the bed of a pickup truck to receive instructions. Then we scatter across several acres of healthy wiregrass, shoulders saddled with canvas bags. I think of the reusable bags I take to the grocery store—symbols of my desire to live in harmony with the earth, but also reminders of the gross inadequacy of my individual efforts. Hauling these pines feels far more satisfying. I sink a hole digger into sand, palm the warm, damp weight of a root ball, and gently press it into the ground. These motions reverberate with meaning: I am giving life to something—not just a tree, but to hundreds of other beings that will depend on this tree for their survival. I look at my dirty hands and feel a conversion taking place, a web of cracks splitting my brittle shell of cynicism.

As an office-bound academic, I often connect to the natural world through books, articles, and philosophical discussions. I inhabit a realm of ideas, where dire predictions from climate scientists, politicians who favor deregulation, and humans' intractable need to consume loom large. But being at Apalachicola Bluffs and Ravines Preserve has shifted my perspective and challenged my paradigm.

Deeply engaging with this place, listening to people who know it and love it well, sleeping on a particular patch of earth and feeling it on my fingertips and lips and in between my toes has given me hope. Maybe it is within our reach to save whole ecosystems. And maybe we make that happen by doing small things (like planting seeds) that are part of small undertakings (like restoring an acre) that are part of bigger initiatives (like managing a preserve) that are part of big movements (like reestablishing 8 million acres of longleaf pine savannah).

I think of something one of my group's student leaders said earlier this week: "I don't see [wilderness] as a separate thing . . . I see us more as a part of it."

Those words struck me as naïve then, but I receive them as wisdom now. In this act of planting a longleaf pine, I am neither an interloper, meddling with what I do not understand, nor a doctor, imposing an alien cure on my helpless patient. Rather, I am part of a complex ecosystem that is slowly healing itself, an ecosystem that includes humans (for the moment, at least.)

The final night of our trip, David Printiss, The Nature Conservancy's North Florida conservation director, treats us to a barbeque in his front lawn, just up the hill from the nursery where we've seeded 130,000 wire-grass plugs.

After the meal, I ask Printiss how he staves off pessimism when confronted with setbacks like Governor Scott's ban on the term "climate change."

He shrugs and reminds me of what they've been able to accomplish in spite of political and systemic challenges: The Nature Conservancy has pioneered ground-cover restoration for the longleaf pine ecosystem—uncharted territory when the site was purchased three decades ago. And what they've learned hasn't just enabled them to reclaim thousands of acres here—it's opened up partnerships and exchanges with publicly owned lands, like the neighboring Torreya State Park and Apalachicola National Forest.

The problem they're wrestling with now, Printiss says, is recruiting people to the field of land management. There's work to be done, but there aren't enough applicants for the available jobs.

Tomorrow, we will drive back to Virginia, soil still caked beneath our fingernails, and I don't know what will happen next. I don't know how many of the seeds we planted will survive long enough to spread fire across these sandhills. I don't know if any of these students will choose to make environmental restoration their life's work. I don't know what the carbon in our atmosphere will do to this preserve or to us or to this planet.

Contemplating the tract of restored habitat in front of me, I look for the wasteland I surveyed five days ago, but I cannot find it. Evening gilds the wiregrass, florets nodding over anthills and gopher tortoise mounds. Birds and toads and crickets sing mightily. Longleaf pines stand at attention, branches adorned with green tassels that conceal silver, heat-deflecting buds. On the horizon to the southeast, the treetops dip low, marking the mouth of a steephead ravine, a portal to an ancient world.

Far-off laughter rises from the backyard, where the students are taking turns on a swing, sailing feet-first over the Apalachicola River basin. I close my eyes, inhale air laced with the scent of approaching rain, and turn to join them.

Vena Cava

Chantel Acevedo

Miami Rail, 2017

You might think my whole life was once 12th Avenue in Hialeah, and at one time, you'd have been right. Hialeah numbers its streets according to its own system, reduced to East and West, bisected by Palm Avenue. It's a remonstrative difference from the rest of Miami-Dade County. For clarity, and because one shouldn't get lost, especially at night, 12th Avenue is called Ludlam Road nearly everywhere else, and if not for the airport slicing it in half, you could take 12th Avenue all the way to the walled lawns of Pinecrest if you wished, leaving Hialeah's strip malls and motels behind.

This crossroad, where 12th Avenue meets 60th Street, was once the epicenter of my life. Just down the block, Palm Springs Middle School rises from the weeds like a Borg cube. The walls weren't always there. Formerly, it was all open courtyards, with a horse statue in the middle, confusing the students who never understood why the school mascot was a Pacer, rarely thought about the horse track on the east side of town, and who never knew that Winston Churchill liked to visit the Hialeah Race Track, or who, for that matter, Winston Churchill even was. I lived on the other side of the P.E. fields, and on the last day of school, early, when the weeds were damp with dew, kids would hide cans of shaving cream in the bushes in front of my house and retrieve them at the end of the day for a shaving cream fight that always ended with the police being called.

Across the street, there in a coral-colored house, lived a butcher, his wife, and their grown son who, one day, forced his parents at gunpoint up into the hot and cramped attic, making them crawl on their bellies, then called the cops on himself. The hostage situation lasted all afternoon. A skinny cop knocked on our door and told us to keep away from the windows, which we did not do.

Up the street, you'll find the pharmacy where my grandmother went to get medicine without prescriptions. The pharmacist, let us call him Suarez, was her friend, and he knew the rising costs of deductibles, understood that factory work sometimes did not come with benefits. My grandmother would bring Suarez biker shorts from the tallér for his teen daughters, and he would give her penicillin, Dimetapp, back when it required a script, Robitussin, and other things. We pronounced them Dee-meh-TAH and Ro-bee-too-SIN, and it was in that house just off of 12th Avenue where I first saw a commercial for those medicines and heard those made-up-anyway words in English for the first time.

My asthma was bad then, and the concoctions that my grandmother and the pharmacist planned for me sometimes made me hallucinate. When I was eight, I thought the water in the faucets had slowed down to molasses. I swear I saw it. I never told anyone, because I thought I was going crazy. When I was ten, an FPL man fell off the top of a telephone pole in our backyard, and snapped his leg in two. I watched him fall, and stood there in a Robitussin haze, unsure I had seen what I had seen, and he had to yell at me no seas una estupida and go get help.

Speaking of crazy, you should know that my grandfather died of Alzheimer's, and that his symptoms were not subtle. One afternoon, he took all of the jewels he had bought for my grandmother over the years, and sold them in that same pharmacy for five dollars. Suarez later claimed that such a thing never happened. But the jewels were gone, and my grandfather clung to that fiver like it was keeping him alive. He lived another twenty years, though for most of that time, he could not swallow on his own or utter a word.

I had my braces tightened once a month farther down 12th Avenue, and Dr. Hoffman was the first Jewish person I ever met. He was very nice, and the braces did not hurt much. His office was next to my childhood dentist, who pulled two of my permanent molars in preparation for the braces. She hitched her foot onto the chair's armrest for leverage and pulled, and pulled, and pulled. She was, perhaps, the millionth Cuban woman I had met and despite the brutality of what she did to me, was also nice. Later, my mother bought me ice cream at "la vaquita" store, also next door.

If I have to explain "la vaquita" to you, then perhaps you shouldn't spend time in Hialeah. What would be the point?

On this same street, a few blocks north of the orthodontist, was my high school. A third of the students came from Hialeah, and we recognized 12th Avenue for what it was—our vena cava. We were the ones who loitered near the art classrooms, the girls who tried out for Danceline because we had learned to shimmy and flash a thigh at all of those quinceañera parties. A third of the students came from Miami Lakes, where a manicured lawn was a sign of godliness. For those few, life presented them with Optimist soccer clubs and Little League, Girl Scouts and Boy Scouts, full-size candy bars at their neighbors' homes at Halloween. A third of the students came from Opa-Locka, arriving in buses that scooped them up before dawn, delivering them, bleary-eyed, to homerooms. Opa-Locka kids hung out on the second floor, where a forty-foot pane of glass stood at their backs, with a view of the gym beyond. When a fist struck the glass, the sound was like a deep, bass drum; all day, all day, music was pounded into that glass, and I remember feeling it in my feet and in my chest. Next to the school was project housing. We all called the buildings "Vietnam," even though most of us could not locate Vietnam on a map, or understood what was happening there when we were all born, or how that war had shaped the world. I don't remember our history teachers ever getting to Vietnam in our lessons. Somehow, the school year always ended sometime after the assassination of Archduke Ferdinand, as if time simply ended there, all of us focused on the trigger in perpetuity, and never the aftermath.

You should know that our valedictorian and salutatorian, our head cheerleader and student council president, were all Miami Lakes children. These children knew things that the rest of us didn't. For example, somehow they knew that P.E. was optional, so that they would have room in their schedules for more AP courses, and that AP courses were worth more in a GPA. The rest of us mostly followed the rules regarding such things, reading them to our parents, who could not always read them in English. So it was that we never, no matter how many straight As we had, could ever catch up.

You might be interested in learning about my college counselor. She wore bottle-thick glasses, and accused me of cheating on my SATs, because my PSATs had been low and I had improved so much over the course of one summer. I told her that perhaps the fact that we took our PSATs in the auditorium, the pages on our laps, our dull pencils poking through the Scantron sheets and into our thighs, had something to do with it. She removed her glasses, licked them to get them clean, like a cat would. When I told her my dreams of going to Mount Holyoke or, barring that, the University of Miami, she suggested I lower my expectations.

You should know that this was a long time ago.

Perhaps much has changed.

However, this I know for certain: the glass pane over the gym is gone—sheetrocked over—and the school at the north end of 12th Avenue is surrounded by a very high fence that is very hard to climb over.

My best friend got married on 12th Avenue, in a banquet hall. She was two hours late to her wedding, and we passed the time wandering the strip mall connected to the banquet hall, checking out the beeper store. My uncle's A/C company was on 12th Avenue. It went under, then was resurrected, then under again, and back, the Lazarus of A/C and heating repair businesses.

Where 68th meets 12th, three teenagers died in a crash when they raced another car in the middle of the day. Faded teddy bears are lashed to the stop signs nearby. They were two boys and a girl. The girl went to my high school, long after I graduated. After her death, her mother stood in the parking lot every day at lunchtime, trying to keep the kids from leaving campus in their cars. She even stood there in the rain, umbrella balanced on her shoulder, her hands raised in the universal sign for "Stop."

Twelfth Avenue will take you to Okeechobee, and there you'll find the megastore, Ñooooo, Que Barato, which sells cheap things and giant duffel bags for trips to Cuba, plus white clothes for the Santero/a in your life. Next door, there is a daycare. My cousin's ex-husband claims they tied him up with a rope there thirty years ago, back before timeouts existed. I have relatives up and down 12th Avenue. There are more Obamacare advertisements in Hialeah than anywhere else on the planet. Hialeah is, in point of fact, Obamacare's number-one city, leading the nation in enrollees. Most everyone I know in Hialeah also voted to Make America Great Again. Irony, which Hialeah has never lacked, is so thick there you might reach out and poke it.

My ninety-year-old abuela lives on 12th Avenue, in a tiny apartment full of Dollar Store picture frames and wind chimes, which she ties to the pulls on her ceiling fan. On hot days, she refuses to turn on her A/C, even though it is included in her rent. She wears scarves in the summer. Her neighbors call her "Abuela," and see her more often than I do, because 12th Avenue is now so far away from me, and you know, at the end of the day, traffic on Le Jeune makes going to Hialeah "a mission," as we like to say.

For fifteen years, I lived in other states, where other streets gathered meaning in the story of my life. My grandmother would sometimes tease, tell me I had become una Americana. I lived in quiet, rural places, and she would compare them to 12th Avenue, which was un peligro, as she always says. Now I am back, and after visiting her one day, I watched as a car struck a pedestrian on 12th Avenue, saw the man roll twice down the street like a sausage on a spit, watched him get up, check his elbows for scrapes, and finish crossing to the other side. The driver did not notice, as he was holding a cell phone with the GPS running, his eyes on the map.

Now, if you were to make a map out of me, then 12th Avenue would have to be drawn down my spine, north to south. The streets and roads would be my veins, the ranch homes with their closed-up garages my capillaries, my hair the clouds of blackbirds murmuring in the sky over the condos, alighting like teeth on telephone wires.

Rolling in the Mud

Sandra Gail Lambert

A Certain Loneliness: A Memoir, 2018

I've never touched earth much. Water, yes. As a child, I unbuckled knee pads and thigh straps to lift legs out of their braces. My skin hissed as it pulled away from the brushed leather thigh cuffs. With braces and crutches left in a jumble off to the side, I crawled into snow-fed lakes with sudden, immense depths or swam in pools until the world acquired a chlorine-rainbowed hue. My legs pushed through the water and expanded into their own natural shape. The abeyance of gravity would smooth the indentations of straps and aluminum rods designed to untwist and make plumb.

These days, I slip out of a wheelchair and into Florida waters. Spring-fed rivers warm or cool depending on the season, and Atlantic waves toss me until the sea floor scrapes against my skin and water burns my lungs. In summertime in the bathtub-warm and gentle Gulf, I lie on my back with my glasses off, stare at the now-blurred, impressionist sky, and float with no effort the way big women can.

But it's not often that I touch earth directly. Sometimes my hands dig at the surface to plant or pull in my yard. More often it is less immediate: still connected, but once removed. A friend digs for me, her shovel hits a root, and I hear the thud of metal and see the sudden strain in her forearms. I search out the narrow reaches of blackwater creeks where leather fern spores bronze against my shoulders. My kayak noses into the high-tide openings in salt marshes until maiden cane tangles the paddle and black needle rush leans in to itch over my knuckles. Driving over the washboard ripple of a dirt road after rain can shake the topography of a landscape into my bones. And now and again, the rasp of littoral grasses at the edge of a lake sounds into the keel of my boat and feathers the back side of my thighs.

The La Chua Trail into Paynes Prairie is one of the places I'm least removed from the earth. Here, I first saw a bald eagle, a lotus in bloom, a whooping crane. I've pushed my wheelchair past 200 alligators lined along the trail, their heads following in slow motion, while friends and I make jokes about looking as little like poodles as possible.

One year when low water levels attracted hundreds of wood storks, I went day after day to see the fluffed necks of the young ones, and it's not unusual for a water moccasin to raise a warning head out of the grass alongside one of my wheels. The Prairie is a reason I moved to Florida.

I first traveled the trail in a manual chair, then in a scooter, and now in a power wheelchair. When I hear the hiss of sand under my wheels, feel the sink and pull, I know to shift my weight and turn onto a clump of grass that congeals the surface and gives traction. I traveled this trail before there were signs or gates. I traveled it before the state built an observation deck with steps instead of a ramp. It blocks the piece of dry ground where I used to perch each winter to look over the marsh and watch thousands of sandhill cranes mix with occasional groups of white pelicans. And now a vista-destroying boardwalk snakes around Alachua Sink, but it is still a place of connection. I still travel here.

All the seasons on Paynes Prairie have touched me. The purple and yellow days are in the spring—swaths of marsh marigold and spikes of pickerel weed. You have to go in the summer to see the lotus, and the June weight of air in my lungs is a comfort even as sweat slicks the vinyl of my armrests and stings along my spine.

September—still summer in Florida—is always a judgment call. Clouds, black and shot through with a metallic green, tower into the sky, and I brace against downdraft winds to watch the last sunlight at the edge of a storm. It races across the Prairie, tinting the oranges from rust to tangerine, the yellows to neon. It is only when lightning strikes close that I can turn away. Full speed, leaning forward over the controls as if that will make the chair go faster, heedless of hips and back, I bounce over the trail to my van. If I've timed it right, I'm closing the doors before the first, fat raindrops turn into a voice-drowning rush against the metal roof.

Once, in the season of government-controlled burns, a sheer curtain line of fire came close, so thin that it barely blurred the view beyond, and it seemed possible to take a single step and be through it. The inner structure of the air changed as ions shifted and crackled the hairs along my arms. It was as if I were on another planet.

Sometimes in the winter there are cold days that make my bones ache. Alligators burrow in the mud to stay warm, the low humidity blues the sky, and egret and ibis white glints against the eyes.

In the late 1990s, the Prairie flooded. It wasn't like in 1873. Then the Alachua Sink that drains the Prairie blocked and stayed that way for almost 20 years until, in a sudden drop, the lake disappeared and left steamboats, waterfront tourist attractions, and thousands of fish stranded. For us, it flooded high and for long enough that water lapped over the outside lanes of the highway that cuts the Prairie in two, and alligators, desperate for any high ground, lay nose up to the traffic.

There were daily reports. Would the road crumble apart? Float away? Crack? I wanted it to. I wanted to witness the Prairie become once again the Great Alachua Savanna. It did not happen.

But I started searching the road for a place to pull over, yank my kayak out from the back of the van, and slip into the water. I planned to leave my empty wheelchair beside the road as a puzzle for the police or State Park rangers. All I had to do was get beyond bullhorn range. It would be worth the ticket just to see what it was they charged me with. But I'm not quick, and my van is not stealthy, so I never tried. Of course, I wasn't the only one thinking this way, and eventually the State Park allowed guided kayak trips. I signed up.

When the day comes, I'm early so it's just Lars and me at the edge of the flood. The water is wonderfully disorienting. The big oak where I usually park my van and start my strolls is at the new shoreline. Lars, the man who literally wrote the book on the Prairie, is unloading all the rental kayaks while I snap and click the gear into place on my own boat. He has to go unlock the gate for the rest of the people. Will I be okay? Yes, I say. And this is part of why I admire Lars; he believes me. He lets me be on my own. This type of respect is usually something I have to fight for, even threaten lawsuits over. Sometimes in groups Lars introduces me as an outdoorswoman. It's my favorite thing that I've ever been called.

He leaves. I'm alone on the Prairie. It is still rising, they say. There is no one else here. I stare at the water and think I see it creep along the trail.

The gate is locked until Lars unlocks it and lets the rest of today's kayak tour in. I don't have long to be alone, but I do have this time. I won't wait. I drop out of my wheelchair and land on the very last of dry earth, at least for today. I scoot on my bottom, pull the kayak, scoot more, pull the kayak. Through my nylon pants, under my bare hands, the ground becomes first cooler, then wet.

This isn't a regular lake edge. No pennywort laps through stalks of arrowhead and bull rush anchored in muck. No buttressed trunks of cypress trees line the shore. This has been high ground for a hundred years. The spiderworts, star and pepper grasses, accustomed to sun-baked sand, are dying under the water, but their roots hold firm in earth that is reluctant to become mud.

Again, my arms lift the weight of my body and this time my palms press through sand into water. The path is becoming lake bottom. I pull the kayak to me and lean against it as a red-tailed hawk screams past. This used to be a dry meadow that provided mice and snakes. It will be again. This lake won't exist forever. These events that have led to me being alone, here, on the ground are as ephemeral. I listen for engines, but it's too soon to expect anyone.

I lie on my back, knees bent. A thin skin of water ripples down it. My legs flop to the side, my hip follows, and now my breasts are against the earth. My body mixes the wilted grasses with the soil. I roll again and my shoulder blades sink into the smoothness of dissolving plantain leaves. I spread my arms and rotting grasses wrap around them. A twist of my head and I'm at eye level with everything I used to wheel over. Another roll farther into the water and wet slides along my ribs and covers my wrists. And now I think about an alligator swimming and searching for dry land.

I reverse direction until my elbows scrape into hard sand and the stiff edges of hedge-nettle and Spanish needle. I lift onto my elbows and look around. I can see for a long ways. There are no alligators. I leave the myth of safety on high ground and roll back into the new mud. I stretch out flat, face up. Am I an agent of erosion? Am I joining water and land? My arms reach over my head until fingertips brush into the loosened fibers of earth and muscles pull in a stretch that I usually only feel in bed. It tugs at my flanks and below my belly where thighs and hips are in an unaccustomed straight line. The underside of both knees aches—a good ache—with extension. My head falls and creates a well of water that laps at my earlobes.

Lars's old van rattles over the gravel. I squirm to sitting, readjust my clothes, pull strands of brown grass off my shoulders, and push the kayak through wilting dog fennel to a floatable depth. I splash the less muddy water over my front to clean up a bit. Leaning on the kayak, I kneel over it and tumble and twist into the seat. My knees are the last part of me pressed into the watery earth of Paynes Prairie.

For hours we kayak through fields of lotus and alongside the sunken steps of the observation tower. Attached to the drowning branches of elderberry, gelatinous balls of frog eggs rock in the slow wake of our boats. I stop paddling. The others are ahead of me. I lean toward the bow to ease my back, and my face lowers over my knees and into the oily plant stains and heavy velvet smell of the shoreline. The kayak, responding to the shifts of my body, the wind, the pull of imperceptible currents, turns itself around. Behind us, where we've just traveled, alligators rise.

I'm home. It's evening. I've hosed the sand and slime off the boat, rinsed the paddle, and untangled rotting morning glory from around the bowline. My body is showered and smells only of oatmeal soap and chlorinated water. Now, I'm going to sprinkle baking soda over the laundry, but I hold the clothes against my nose one last time. The water will rise over where I was today and then fall away.

What will the path look like when it emerges? Will there have been time for sagittaria to root and grow tall over the water? Will the purple, white, and yellow of bladderworts skim the surface to either side? As I roll over a barely dry trail, shifting away from the patches of mud that remain, will my front wheels dip and lift out of the lingering physical memory of my body? Perhaps lotus will have spread close to the path. I'll perch at the edge of my seat, anchor one arm around the backrest, and lean over the water that remains to reach the oval petals and touch into the swirl of orange-stalked stamens at their center. I close the washing machine lid and set the rinse water to hot.

How Can You Be Mad at Someone Who's Dying of Cancer?

Deesha Philyaw

Full Grown People, 2015

How can you be mad at someone who's dying of cancer? It helps if you don't yet know she's dying, if you think the doctors are just trying one more thing. It helps if she is your mother and if she's just driven you crazy your whole life, but insists on a kind of love that leaves you unable to breathe and sick to your stomach from her phone calls or from the mere thought of her visiting you or you visiting her. It helps if she is obsessed with you, her only child, because she believes God sent you to her teenage self to love her since no one else did. It helps if she pours her whole life into you, but you never asked her to, and you would have rather she not, just so you could fucking breathe and dress conservatively and keep the pasta separate from the sauce and breastfeed your baby and buy organic, without her judging you from the valley of her insecurities.

All of that helps you to get mad at someone who is dying of cancer, especially when she doesn't seem to be doing everything she possibly can to keep herself alive.

"The church was selling fish dinners today."

"You shouldn't be eating fried foods."

"Oh, girl. I pulled the fried part off."

But what about fruits and vegetables? Whole grains? But I know the answer to that. Cancer is no match for five decades of emotional and cultural eating. So I shut my mouth because the last time I tried to talk about what was broken in me-her-us, she accused me of always using "big words and psychological terms," when in fact I had used no words larger than, "I can't do this with you anymore. I'm calling a cab, and I'm leaving." My college education and my intellect were apparently weapons I wielded to intimidate her. One day out of the blue when I was in my 30s, she said, "I finally found the word to describe the way you made me feel your whole life: intimidated."

I think the problem started when I was born. My mother said, "I thought you were going to be dark like me with chinky eyes and wavy hair. Like a doll." Alas, I was born medium-brown, bald, with huge eyes not associated with a racial slur. "Your eyes were so big that for the longest time, they would just roll around because you couldn't focus them," my mother said. "I burst into tears when I saw you. And your hands were so tiny. Until you got pregnant, I always thought that meant you wouldn't be able to have kids."

Please don't ask me to explain that last part. I have no idea what my hands and my fertility have to do with each other. I do know that I wasn't what my mom was expecting. She wanted a dark chocolate doll that would grow up to make the same choices she would have made if she'd had the doll's options in life. A doll that liked all the same things she liked—bright-colored clothing, the right amount of condiments and paprika in her potato salad, makeup.

Oh, the makeup! So when I was in the eighth grade and about to turn 13, many of the girls in my grade wanted to wear makeup. About half their mothers allowed them to. The other half made up their faces in the bathroom at school in the morning and scrubbed it off at some point before getting on the bus at the end of the day. Lucky me, I had one of those makeup-permitting mothers. Unlucky for her, she had a daughter who couldn't give two shits about makeup. It just seemed to me like a lot of effort and for no good reason. But as my 13th birthday approached, my mom was stuck on the idea that a cute little pouch filled with my own cosmetics would make the perfect gift. Meanwhile, a stack of V. C. Andrews books was my idea of the perfect gift. But according to my mother, that wasn't a "real" gift. To hell with the fact that this was *my* birthday. She was determined to get me a real gift and it would be makeup.

"I don't want makeup. But thank you."

"Don't you remember how nice you looked at James's wedding when I let you wear makeup?" I had been eleven when my uncle, my mom's younger brother, got married, and while I hadn't been made up against my will, I hadn't asked for makeup.

"Yes, but I don't want to wear makeup. Thank you, though."

"But why not?"

"Because . . . just because I don't."

"Well, I wish my mama had let me wear makeup when I was your age."

But. I'm. Not. You.

"I don't want to wear makeup."

"No, really. You should," my mother said, fixing her eyes hard on me. "You should."

And it was that last "you should" that did it. I don't mean that I relented; I didn't start wearing makeup regularly until around 11th grade. But that "you should" crushed me. It crushed the microscopic part of me that dared to think that my "big for her age" self was maybe kinda a little bit cute and sort of not too fat. "You should" meant that makeup would make me look better, more presentable, less homely, more like I belonged to my gorgeous mother.

My mother was one of the most beautiful women I've ever seen. I actually preferred her without makeup. Her beauty didn't need any help. She had a glorious 'fro when glorious 'fros were in, the first time around. And her smile . . . My Lord. The woman had perfect lips and perfect teeth, and together, they were brilliant. And until loneliness, depression, and her changing metabolism took its toll, my mother had what folks back then called a "brick house" figure, so named for the popular R&B song by The Commodores.

"You should" was my mother's go-to tactic for shaming me into liking what she liked, and caring about what she cared about. As in, I should care what people would think of me if I didn't dress or carry myself a certain way, i.e., like her. My mother cared a lot about appearances, literally. Overwhelmed by mother's obsession with how others might find me lacking, I became 10 times more self-conscious than your typical self-conscious teen. It was debilitating, and I was damn-near 35 years old before I realized that most people didn't size me up critically the minute I entered a room; they were probably too busy trying to get free of their own mother-induced neuroses to care if my clothes were wrinkled or how my hair looked.

Twenty or so birthdays later, and a few years into my mother's cancer diagnosis, I finally got up the nerve to tell her how much that "you should" had hurt and how I had carried that hurt into adulthood and how her shaming me over the years had contributed to us not having the kind of relationship she said she wanted us to have.

Her response? "Huh. I don't remember that at all."

Which is why I shouldn't have been surprised by her reaction later to the whole stolen ring thing, which became Reason #14 Why You Might Be Mad at Someone with Cancer.

But before I get into that, this is the part where I pause to make sure you don't think my mother was a horrible person or a bad mother. She was neither of those things. This is important and needs to be said because we don't allow mothers to have done some shitty things in the course of their parenting career and still get credit for the good they did. In our cultural consciousness, either mothers are saints or we're driving our minivan full of kids into the river. And in the final tally of who I am because of my mother, I believe she did far more good than harm. She was a loving mother who sacrificed for me, and I always knew that my needs and many of my wants were her priority. If I am generous, hardworking, hospitable, responsible, and a person of integrity, I owe it in large part to my mother's example and guidance. Even in her flaws, she had raised me to do as she said, not as she did.

She also raised me, ironically enough, to speak up for myself. But I guess she just intended for me to do this at school and with other people besides her. At any rate, this knack for being my own advocate came in handy in sophomore year of high school when I got straight A's for the first three grading quarters, and then all A's and a B in gym class in the last quarter. I was livid. How dare the gym teacher, of all people, fuck up my 4.0!

I went to see the girls' dean of students, who had taken me under her wing, but she wasn't in her office that day. Another administrator was there and she did her best to calm me down. She listened as I rattled off all the reasons that this B was some bullshit. Ultimately, my grade didn't get changed, but what did happen is that this administrator remembered me and my righteous indignation. So a month or so later, when our local congressman's office contacted her to recommend a rising junior who was mature and academically talented enough to spend the first half of the coming school year living and working on Capitol Hill as a page in the U.S. House of Representatives, this administrator recommended me.

The day I was due to arrive at the page dorm also happened to be my 16th birthday. My mother had been eager for this day for many years, because it would also be the day that she gave me one of her prized possessions: a gold ring shaped like a rose with a stone at the center of it that may or may not have been a diamond. When I was 5, a guy she had dated had given her this ring. I knew from overhearing my mom's conversations with friends that this guy was a thief. And yet, for 11 years my mother had worn this ring and gushed to me about how when I turned 16, this stolen property would be mine, and then one day, I would give it to my daughter (if I had one . . . you know, with my small hands and all), and my daughter would give it to her daughter . . .

This was my mother's attempt to create a family heirloom. But the things that my mother gave me that I want to pass on to my daughters can't be placed in a ring box, or any box. They are things of spirit and heart. But my mother didn't treasure these gifts. When she was dying, I told her how much I treasured them, but that only added to her grief that she had, in her words, "wasted so much time on us, on things that didn't really matter."

But she didn't have that insight in 1987. So, as ceremoniously as you can be in the page dorm, my mother presented me with the ring. I acted excited because I knew that that was what she wanted, but all I kept thinking was, "This ring was stolen." And I wore the ring for exactly 16 years and nine months.

The day I took the ring off and never wore it again, I was in Florida with my kids, visiting my mother. About four years earlier, she had been diagnosed with breast cancer. When she had called to tell me, I'd been a few months into a self-imposed hiatus from her. I'd finally decided that I couldn't take her guilt trips and criticisms of my life and choices anymore. I needed a break from her. I told her not to call or e-mail me, and not to expect to hear from me. Indefinitely. I can't remember what the straw was that broke the camel's back, but I do remember that a year or so before the hiatus, she'd sent me a pair of burgundy jeans (she was always sending me clothes that I never wore) and got upset when I said that I hadn't worn them and had no intention of wearing them because I'd asked her countless times to stop sending me clothes (1) because I was an adult, and (2) because the clothes she sent weren't my style. "But your style is boring!" she'd said. And this was the argument in which she denied ever being critical of me.

So. Something else happened after that, and I decided to take a break from her. And then she got the cancer diagnosis, and fuck. So I ended the hiatus and learned everything I could about cancer and how we could save her life. It didn't take long for me to realize that I couldn't save her life; I couldn't even get her to change her eating habits. So I began to mourn her while she was still alive.

June 7, 2005, was a ridiculously hot day in Jacksonville, Florida, which is saying a lot. But my mom wanted to take my daughters to the zoo during our weeklong visit, and I agreed, even though I wasn't really up for it. My mother had told me that her doctors were going to try one more treatment, but they weren't sure if they could do anything else for her after that. My beloved grandmother, who had helped my mom raise me, had died from ovarian and colon cancer that January. I was in the middle of a separation, heading to divorce. And the last thing I wanted to do was spend the day out in the heat. Needless to say, I was miserable, but of course my mother wanted to invite a drunken neighbor and her grandson to go with us to the zoo. In the monkey habitat, the neighbor kept screaming at the monkeys to shut up. I wanted to push her into the tiger pit.

On the ride home, my period started, just to cap off such a glorious day. I had to stop off at CVS. I left my mom and my kids in the air-conditioned rental SUV, so that I could at least be alone in the store. I picked up what I needed and stood in line. Someone behind me tapped me on the shoulder.

"Excuse me, but you just cut in front of me in the line."

"Oh, my god! I'm so sorry!" I said to the woman behind me. And when I said this, I grabbed the edge of the counter because I thought I would faint. How had I missed this entire line of people?

The woman looked down at my hand and said, "What a beautiful ring!"

It was the stolen rose ring my mother had given me. "Oh. Thank you," I said.

The woman continued. "You know, I had a ring just like that. Back in the '70s. I bought it with my very first paycheck, but . . ."

No. No. *Nononononono.*

" . . . somebody broke into my apartment and stole it."

"Oh. Well . . . My mother gave me this one . . ."

I wanted to go outside and drag my mother out of that SUV and . . . And what? She had cancer. How can you be mad at someone who has cancer?

I thought about giving the woman the ring. "Here's your ring, ma'am. My mother suffers from some kind of condition that made her think that not only accepting a stolen ring as a gift was a good idea, but that she should also give it to me to pass down through the generations of our family. Please understand."

But I couldn't risk getting arrested.

I felt like shit. I felt like shit and I hadn't done anything wrong.

Except accept stolen property.

From my mother.

But it was only because I didn't want her to feel bad.

The woman kept chatting about how she'd lived in Jacksonville until the early 80s but then moved to Dallas where she was a nurse (I think). She was home visiting her mother, who, as it turned out, had cancer. I told her that my mother also had cancer, and we gave each other that knowing "Fuck cancer" look. And then she let me go ahead of her anyway in the check-out line and wished my mother well. I wished her mother well too and then headed back to the SUV.

"There was a woman in there in the check-out line who saw the ring you gave me, and it turns out your boyfriend stole it from her all those years ago. It was *her* ring!"

"Hmmm," my mother said. "Small world."

A little over two weeks later, I was back home in Pittsburgh when I got the call that my mother had been hospitalized. She was in so much pain that the doctors didn't expect her to survive the night. But she did, and when I arrived the next day, having caught the first flight I could after getting my kids situated with their dad, I went straight to the hospital. When I walked into her room, my mom's best friend was there, and my mom beamed at her and said, "Oh, look! Deesha came!"

As if there had been a question of whether I would or not, continuing the pity narrative that my mother had kept up among her friends that I was just too busy with my own life to be concerned about her. I found out later, after she'd died, that she had known her cancer was at Stage 4 for several months before telling me. She had told everyone but me. But she didn't tell her friends that she hadn't told me. So when they asked why I hadn't come down to see her, she'd say, "Oh, you know . . . she's just so busy with her own life." So of course I looked like an asshole of a daughter, and everyone felt extra sorry for my mother because she had cancer *and* an asshole for a daughter.

In the two months I spent in Jacksonville when my mom was dying, I had to contend with people thinking I'd been a negligent daughter, while also tending to all of my mother's complicated affairs and trying to see my kids whenever their dad was able to fly them down to me. My kids were 6½ and 1½ at the time.

My ex had known me, and by extension, my mother, since I was 18 years old. He knew better than anyone how much grief my relationship with my mother had caused me over the years. When she had contacted him behind my back during the hiatus, hoping to make a surprise visit for my birthday . . . *during the fucking hiatus* . . . my then-husband had gently explained why that would be a terrible idea. "It's like when you hold a bar of soap in the shower," he'd told her. "If you hold on too tightly, the soap will slip away."

And I had slipped away from my mother, long before she slipped away from me in death. But then I came back, in the ways that I could, in the time that she had left. On a yellow legal pad, I made long lists of things she wanted and things she wanted done after her death. How to distribute the vast contents of her costume jewelry collection, who to give the canned goods in her pantry. A big party at the hospice center for her and a hundred of her closest friends. Directions to pay her best friend's utility bills for a year. Permission to give her brothers absolutely nothing since, in her estimation, she had given them enough money already over the years because she'd felt guilty telling them "no."

"Don't let them or anyone make you feel guilty for doing what you want to do," my mother told me. "Live your life."

I had waited my whole life to hear those words from my mother. I ached that they came too late for us to both fully enjoy the aftermath together, but I'm so very glad they came. Her words freed me.

My mother was lucid for most of her time in hospice. And not just lucid, but often hilarious. There was that a-hundred-person party at the hospital adjacent to the hospice center. My mother insisted on doing her own makeup and having a decorative cover for her colostomy bag. Someone alerted the local news, and they sent a camera crew and a reporter who asked my mother, "How does this celebration make you feel?"

And my mother, her voice heavy with Dilaudid, said, "Popular."

And there was that day a childhood friend stopped by. He told my mother that he'd always had a crush on her, growing up. She'd been skinny and asthmatic as a kid, but he thought she was beautiful. "And you still are beautiful," he told her.

After he left, my mom said to me, "Fine time for him to tell me alla that. But girl, look. I'm on my deathbed, and I still got it goin' on."

This is why I felt my mother would not mind how I dressed for her funeral. I had become obsessed with not sweating at the funeral, so I found this cocktail dress, above-the-knee, sleeveless, more "after 5" than "your mother's funeral." And I wore backless heels that were anything but conservative. And I think I strutted up to my mother's casket because you can't do anything but strut in heels like that.

And I'm pretty sure my critics among my mother's friends did not approve of my attire, but I didn't care. I didn't sweat and I didn't faint and I survived the day. And I've survived the many days since then, knowing that my mother died fully aware of how much I loved her, how much I had always loved her, despite all of the fights and frustration.

I wish that I hadn't needed my mother's permission to live my life. I wish that I had just been able to live it and ignore her criticisms, without having to hold her at arm's length. I wish I had been strong and confident enough in myself to do that while she was alive, instead of having that strength and confidence ushered in by her death.

My mother's death hasn't changed what I remember about my relationship with her, but it has caused me to filter the memories through a lens of understanding, gratitude, and humility. I have to show my mother this grace if for no other reason than I hope my own daughters will do the same for me. My mother's utter obliviousness to her parenting missteps forces me to recognize the likelihood of my own misinterpretation of my parenting actions and intentions. What I see as well-intentioned and helpful, my daughters could very well experience as overbearing and judgmental. What I offer as guidance might feel to them like pressure and shaming. I can't dictate their experience, and I won't tell them how to feel. I can only communicate my desire for them to be free to be who they are, even when I can't relate. And I can keep the lines of communication open so that they can tell me what they need from me in order to thrive, even when it's hard for me to hear. I can do the very best I can with what I know, which, I believe, is what my mother did.

Returning to Hopelessness

Bill Maxwell

CRESCENT CITY—I came of age in 1963, when I graduated from all-black Middleton High School in Crescent City. By "came of age," I mean when I started to believe I could control much of my fate. After all, the civil rights movement had matured, Jim Crow ostensibly was in retreat, and passage of the Civil Rights Act seemed imminent.

The new legislation was being hailed as a potential life-changer for the South's disenfranchised peoples, especially blacks. It would end segregation in public places and outlaw employment discrimination on the basis of race, color, religion, sex, or national origin. And the March on Washington for Jobs and Freedom that summer gave us hope like we had never experienced.

Less than a year later, when I was a freshman at all-black Wiley College in Marshall, Texas, the Civil Rights Act became the law of the land. I returned home for the summer hoping to see significant changes. I did not.

The dehumanizing practices my grandfather, a Pentecostal minister, referred to as "soul stuff," had not changed. The two locally owned diners still would not serve blacks. "Breaking bread with people is personal," my grandfather said. We still could not try on clothes in stores. We still had to use the cramped balcony in the theater. Sitting skin-to-skin was too personal.

Blacks and whites still could not swim together at Lake Stella. We had separate beaches. The fear, of course, was that black boys would ogle white girls, perhaps even rape them. We resented the portrayal. Blacks and whites still washed clothes in separate "White Only" and "Colored Only" sections of the laundromat.

What I quickly learned was that desegregation did not automatically translate into respect and acceptance. The old ways remained in the hearts and souls of white residents who always had held power. And we blacks held on to our old resentments and fears.

The first sign of substantive racial progress in Crescent City came a couple of years later when the county school board decided to follow the federal mandate to desegregate the schools. A new unified high school was built in Crescent City, and children who had not spoken to another became acquaintances. Black and white athletes became teammates for the first time.

Most surprisingly, white residents did not insist on using the former all-white school's nickname, the Rebels. Waving the Confederate flag during games also was discontinued. The new school's sports nickname became the Raiders. It was a development that renewed hopes of real racial progress.

Over time, the school hired its first black principal, residents elected the first black council member, and the first black police chief was hired.

During my recent visit, I did not experience a single act of overt racism, the kind I experienced growing up, when black men took off their hats and stepped off the sidewalk to let white women pass, when "yes, sir," and "yes, ma'am" were expected when addressing white people.

Overt racism has been replaced by benign neglect, which is more insidious. Few blacks and whites live as neighbors. I spent a lot of time in the predominantly black communities of Babylon, Denver, Long Station, Rossville, Union Avenue, and Whitesville. When I was a kid, these were vibrant places where hardworking people reared families. Most families are gone, and most of the old houses are uninhabitable.

Elected officials apparently have disinvested from these places. Most of the streets remain unpaved and some have potholes the size of swimming pools. During hard rains, some streets are impassable. Nothing indicates that these black neighborhoods are part of the municipal or county improvement plans.

Unfortunately, such neglect threatens the area's continued viability because the most important resource, young people, leave and do not return to live and work. When I left in 1963, the population was roughly 1,000. Today, more than 50 years later, the population hovers around 1,600, and the medium resident age is 43.4 years.

Human conduct is not the only reason for the fading hopes of Crescent City blacks. For generations, citrus was the major source of employment, giving blacks steady income and security. Freezing temperatures, beginning in the 1960s and continuing through the late 1980s, wiped out the industry, hurting blacks more than anyone else. Fern growing remains a dependable source of income for many residents, but it does not offer the widespread benefits of citrus production.

When the fruit trees died, many blacks packed up and left the area altogether. Others stayed but soon found themselves struggling to make ends meet. Today, blacks here are more disenfranchised than ever, and the few I spoke with on the street said they had nowhere else to go. They languish on the porches and stoops of dilapidated houses and under trees, hoping someone needing a few hours of day labor will come along.

I told three men, each in his late 20s, that they did not have to live the way they were. They could choose to do something different. I told them about my generation of blacks who grew up here during Jim Crow, when racial segregation was the law. They grinned and rolled their eyes as I talked.

I told them how we thrived intellectually in our all-black school, how our teachers insisted that we learn, how they disciplined us with our parents' consent. The bitter truth, I said, was that segregation, although bad in the eyes of many, made us independent and self-reliant. It forced us to become critical thinkers.

It could happen today, I said.

We were taught the difference between "positive and negative role models." One of our teachers said that "knowing the difference could make all the difference." We therefore studied the lives of blacks who succeeded against the odds. Their aspirations became ours, their accomplishments our goals.

We were lucky to have teachers who knew, for example, about the singular greatness of Asa Philip Randolph, who was born in Crescent City in 1889. They discussed him in our classes, and he became a prime role model for many of us. We were taught that if we emulated him, that if we made education a priority, we would be insulated from the perpetual humiliations of racism.

We learned that Randolph founded the Brotherhood of Sleeping Car Porters in 1925 and led it until 1968. He persuaded the Pullman Company to negotiate with the black labor union. He persuaded President Franklin Roosevelt to open defense jobs to blacks during World War II, and he persuaded President Harry Truman to desegregate the military after the war ended.

Randolph is honored on a Florida Historical Marker in Crescent City in front of the Union Bethel AME Church where his father was the pastor. The marker was installed in 2005.

The paradox is that the marker quotes one of Randolph's greatest insights: "Salvation for a race, nation or class must come from within. Freedom is never granted; it is won, it is never given; it is exacted."

Whenever I return to Crescent City, I visit the marker, always feeling Randolph's presence. Others of my generation also visit. For us, it is a living reminder that learning and self-reliance are key to the survival of black people in America.

I asked several black kids who live near the marker if they know who Asa Philip Randolph was and why he is important. One was familiar with his name. Someone will have to teach these kids and others that they have the innate potential to be successful, like this black man, in spite of racism.

Life in the Shade of Modern Babel

Jan Becker

Sliver of Stone Magazine, 2016

I have a clear memory of a road trip my family took across the country when I was 11. The idea behind the trip was to traverse the wide waistline of America in imitation of the perfect families we saw loading up their station wagons on television. My mother was at the wheel, speeding through the desert in California. The landscape was flashing by the windows, grey, brown, and barren. A few dry tumbling weeds rolled alongside the road. My younger brother Danny was poking me in the backseat, and my younger sister, Kim, who was still wearing diapers, was sitting up front on my stepfather's lap, fussing. It was hot and there was no air-conditioning in the car, so the windows were all rolled down. When Kim began to scream, my stepfather grabbed her by the back of her dress and hung her out the window like a rag doll. That moment is frozen in my mind, the way the sunlight caught in her red hair as the ground streaked beneath her at over eighty miles an hour. The fabric of her dress was so thin, if it had torn, if the seams had unraveled, she would have fallen to her death.

What is perhaps the strongest about that memory is the silence, how the air rushing at her face stole my sister's voice away, how my brother stopped poking me in the backseat, and I stopped protesting, shocked that my stepfather had breached the line into savagery. Even my mother was silent in that moment, though every impulse must have been pushing her to panic. Slowly, she pulled over to the side of the road. Only when my sister was back in the car, safely seated between my brother and me, did Mom let loose a belly roar and coldcock my stepfather with a right hook to the jaw. That snap of fist against jaw broke the silence we were all trapped in, that moment when the fabric keeping my sister alive seemed impossibly thin.

My boyfriend's former roommate, Joe DiFulvio, told me that he saw the devil staring at him one night in a live oak on the shores of Crystal Lake in Pompano Beach, Florida. "Pure evil staring at me from the top of the tree," he said. When I asked him what kind of impact that had on his life, he shrugged, "I was smoking some really high-test weed and was a little drunk on good beer, so it didn't stick with me." Joe hasn't seen the devil since he moved north a few years ago. As skeptical as I am about such things, as much as I want to say that it must have just been some killer pot, that Joe is an unreliable witness, I believe that he felt something outside by the lake. I have seen that sort of evil at Crystal Lake.

Evil is not a supernatural force. It is not a horned devil with a pitchfork. It is more familiar than a goat-footed monster with a Van Dyke. Evil is the blunt end of a cudgel, a knife's edge, a set of fingers wrapped around a throat. It is making the decision to traipse across the dividing line between benevolence and savagery, and to embrace violence. In that instant, sanity falls away like a discarded token that has lost its value.

I moved to Pompano Beach from Upstate New York in 2009 to attend a graduate program in creative writing, and to be closer to my long-term but faraway boyfriend. I met Matt in Binghamton, New York, his hometown. He left Binghamton for Florida a long time ago. Matt works as a chef in one of the many country clubs in Boca Raton. He has been living here, in the same apartment, for the past twenty-three years. He has never considered moving to an updated place with modern countertops and newer floors, one with a kitchen that doesn't make him curse in frustration when he tries to cook at home. We could afford a mortgage, and a small house with a yard, but Matt is comfortable here. This is his home.

"Home" is a foreign notion to me, something I never really thought I could have for myself. I grew up in the Marine Corps, in a series of houses on military bases, none of them home, none of them unique. Each bore the same white walls and boxlike shape. Every time we left these houses, the unit was inspected to make sure that we left nothing of ourselves behind. I moved to Florida to build something better; I also moved here to get away from something I am learning is impossible to escape. I grew up with violence all around me. It was common to see women shopping in the commissary in big, dark sunglasses to hide their blackened eyes. I can remember the bruises and broken bones of beaten women and children on every base I lived. As an adult in the civilian world—one who moved around a lot—I have never lived in a town without a murder statistic.

At first, this apartment on Crystal Lake was just another temporary shelter, a characterless building to house me, but three years after moving here, the place is beginning to become comfortable, and I find myself calling it home.

Matt is the first man I have been able to tolerate for any length of time. He has a gentle disposition, but is also quietly strong. He laughs out loud when he sees a baby in a restaurant. He checks my tire pressure weekly and waxes my car. He supports my decision to be a student at an age when most people are trying to build a retirement fund. He also works very long hours. This gives me a lot of time to accomplish my own goals. In the back of our apartment, set aside just for me, I have what Virginia Woolf said every woman needs, a room of my own to write in, with a beautiful view of the lake, and a door that locks tightly if I need to be alone.

It was Matt who urged me to look into the history of Crystal Lake. "Some crazy things have happened out there," he told me, "people have died." I began to look at the history, and at the lake itself, so I could understand this place I call home now.

Crystal Lake was created when, during the housing boom in South Florida in the 1950s, the land had to be dug away and used as filler for construction sites. Advertisements in *Life* magazine lured Northern retirees to the area with the promise of sunshine and key lime pie–colored homes. The advertisements were so seductive, the promise of good life so tempting, that many of the first homeowners in Pompano Beach bought their homes based on pretty pictures.

One cannot dig too deeply in Florida without hitting water. In place of a flat patch of land, a lake emerged. Because big machines dug out the lake, it is shaped strangely. In satellite images, it looks like an arm stretched upward gripping a square meat cleaver, ready to swing. The length of the arm, from the tip of the cleaver to shoulder is about two and a half miles long. At ground level, one can see both shores across the width of the lake, but not end to end. There are no clear walking paths; it's not an easy place to explore, except by boat. In the summer months, there is a frenzy of activity on the lake; Jet Skis compete with fishermen angling for peacock bass. A water-ski academy holds lessons on the lake. Families strap their screaming children to inflatable rafts and drag them across the water with speedboats. On Sunday mornings, a dog trainer takes his retrievers out for lessons in fetch, and his shouts of "good boy" resound over the din of traffic making its way toward the turnpike.

Sixty years after the construction of homes began, most of the original retirees have died or packed up and moved to nursing homes. Around the time the retirees began to leave, Brazil was on the verge of an economic collapse, and many people fled to find work in South Florida. Crystal Lake is far enough away from the big cities of Miami and Fort Lauderdale that the rent is affordable. So the Brazilians moved here. There are little ethnic pockets all over the area. In mine, the language is Portuguese. During World Cup games, the four-story building I live in shakes with cheers every time team Brazil scores. On Sundays, the air is filled the sounds of reggae-samba, and the smells of barbecued picanha.

The name "Crystal Lake" conjures a series of movies from my teenage years. When I first heard about this place, I thought of Jason Voorhees in a hockey mask at a campground on a dark Friday the 13th. There is no Camp Crystal Lake in Pompano Beach, though. Instead, we have Crystal Lake Golf Club. The golf course is established and landscaped with mature pines, but the old country club is beginning to decay. Construction crews are preparing the clubhouse for demolition at the same time they build a new one back from the road. Vandals have punctuated the walls of a former outdoor reception area in fluorescent orange paint with an advertisement for "Ass Rides." The maintenance crews have tried repeatedly to cover the graffiti with white paint, but it eventually bleeds through the whitewash.

The first time I visited Matt in Florida, he took me to the outdoor reception area he called "Club Caligula" for a late-night tango in a tropical canopy of palm leaves and white twinkling lights. We danced there, under an archway decorated with white ribbons where couples said their wedding vows. Now, we have to find other places to tango. Club Caligula has become a tangled jungle of tropical plants, a perfect litter box for a colony of feral cats. Where the floor was once brick, it is now broken turf, littered with hypodermic needles and the makeshift beds of homeless people, uprooted from their tent cities in the mangroves along the highway exit.

Across Crystal Lake from us is a series of commercial complexes and RV storage parks. Above the industrial buildings, the Central County Landfill (we call it Mount Trashmore) rises 225 feet above the lake, billowing clouds of smoke from the incinerator. On calm days, the cloud of smoke hangs rotten with the tinge of methane or, if the DEA is incinerating seized cargo, a hint of marijuana and cocaine. A steady stream of loaded trucks travels the road up the side of the landfill day and night, building a modern Babel.

In the daytime when the Brazilians are off at work and I am home, the residential area of the lake hosts a bucolic scene that often distracts me from writing. Iguanas sun themselves on the shores. Moorhens swim about the water, making squeaky dog-toy noises. Anhinga spearfish in the lake and then, full-bellied, stretch their wings out to dry. In the sky, osprey and turkey vultures circle. Occasionally a brown pelican or a great blue heron flies overhead. Diving ducks bob below the water in search of some protein. In the trees along the lake, squirrels clamber about, upsetting the roosting doves who "coo-coo" in disgust. Seagulls congregate in the water and along the docks by the water, splashing any solid surface with splats of white graffiti.

I spend my evenings spying on courting couples on the wooden bench on the dock, holding hands, moving closer to one another each day as the romances progress, until they are lumped together in a single inseparable unit.

In the spring, the Muscovy ducks began their mating rituals. First, there is a series of duels, where the male ducks engage in combat, trying to break their opponents' wings. The loud chuffing and shuffling sounds of feather on feather, wing beating against wing, signal that the romances have begun. These are big wrestling birds, some more than 20 pounds, pumped up on discarded pasteles and lasagna. Their fights are so violent that a pair of dueling drakes will often roll into the water and continue their combat there without pausing to orient themselves to the new terrain. Once they have secured dominance, the mating dance ensues and when a hen is lured, the drake pins her to the ground, stomps on her wings and back, and finishes the whole deed in about 35 seconds. The only evidence of this brutal conception by rape is the emergence of fluffy ducklings waddling near the water several weeks later. Except for the ducks—and the humans—it is a peaceful place.

My search through the news archives from the *Sun-Sentinel* for deaths on Crystal Lake reveals that Matt is correct; people have died on the lake. I count 16 people, starting in 1967, when a 17-year-old student athlete drowned trying to swim across the lake. Most of the deaths have been from drowning, but a few have been unusual.

In 1984, Anna McGary and her niece took a scuba class on the lake. Anna became entangled in the hydrilla weeds along the shore and lost her mouthpiece. After two days of searching the lake, divers found her body. Her tank still had oxygen in it. Her mouthpiece was dangling by her side. She was one month pregnant with her first child.

In May of 1992, an angler on the lake reeled in what he thought was an extraordinarily large fish. When he pulled his line in, he discovered he had hooked the decomposing body of Michele Bulla, an unemployed Texan who moved to Broward County six months earlier. The Broward County Medical Examiner's Office listed the cause of death as drowning.

In 2001, Leon Resnick was testing a custom Yamaha watercraft at speeds of up to 55 mph. His coworker from Riva Yamaha turned to get a radar gun to clock the speed. When he turned back, Resnick was gone. He had been struck in the face by a 15-pound flying Muscovy duck, and died instantly from his injuries.

People also die right here, in the building I live in. In 1999, the apartment next door caught on fire. Before Joe DiFulvio saw the devil, he saw flames from next door, curling through the windows of his bedroom. Matt sounded the fire alarm, then broke the neighbor's kitchen window. He tried to open the kitchen door, but the smoke was too intense for him to gain entry. That night, two other large fires were burning in Pompano Beach and it took the fire truck close to a half hour to respond. While they were waiting for the firemen, Matt tried to break in and save the people he knew were asleep inside. When the firefighters finally got here and climbed the three flights of stairs to our floor, Matt was certain no one had survived.

Miraculously, the woman who lived there did survive the fire, but her husband perished. I have seen an old VHS recording of the news report that night. In it, Matt is red-faced and anxious, frantic that his home has been threatened, that someone he waved to everyday could leave his wife alone with nothing but wreckage.

Once, in the common area behind our apartment building, I watched a group of teenage girls attending a funeral reception for one of the girls' mothers. At the time, I thought it was a family reunion. The parking lot was filled with out-of-state cars and everyone was wearing their Sunday best. After most of the visitors went home that day, the girls all jumped into Crystal Lake, holding hands, fully clothed. One shouted out, "Do it for your Mom," as they ran into the space between sky and water. When they were finished swimming, they all pulled down their pants and pissed on the dock in the rain. The girl's mother was 42 years old. She had a sudden catastrophic stroke. Her husband told me this as I checked my mail one afternoon shortly after the rainy funeral reception. A few days later, I saw the widower and his daughter loading a U-Haul with their possessions in an effort to move to a new home, one less filled with memories of a dead woman. These deaths in our building and those out on the lake are a reminder that no matter how careful we are, Matt and I could lose each other in an instant.

I did not live on Crystal Lake very long before I began to believe Joe DiFulvio's tale of the devil in the live oak. It wasn't the fire, or the funeral reception or any of the strange accidents that convinced me Joe had seen something that filled him with terror. The night I turned 40, I saw something that, unlike Joe's devil, I can't shake loose from my memory. That night, at a Korean barbecue with friends, I consumed several carafes of sake and came home in a mood to relax. I went out on the balcony to look at the water, and to ponder the meaning of entering my fourth decade.

On the other side of the lake, I saw what I thought was a boat entering the water. This is not unusual; Crystal Lake is dotted with boat launches. Often, fishermen launch late at night and cast in the dark. Occasionally, a group of late-night water-skiers run their boats around the lake, accompanied by loud disco music that blares across the water. This boat had headlights though, and did not appear to be taking a straight path across the water. It floated for a moment, sank, and drifted to the left. The lights from the submerged craft were eerie, almost faerie-like as they dimmed out and died. I didn't think much of the strange boat I saw that night until almost two weeks later when I saw the police cars and tow trucks milling about the industrial park, pulling a car from the water.

Just the day before, on April 5, 2010, a local 63-year-old man named Munawar Toha held a press conference where he begged for help locating his missing wife, Surya. She had come from Jakarta, Indonesia, to South Florida to build a home for her family. At the press conference, police became suspicious at Toha's behavior; he was contrite, but also combative and cocky, first crying, and then angry. He claimed he had no idea where his wife was, even though no one had asked. He begged Surya to come home. She was a good mother. Their children needed her.

Toha reported his wife missing on March 24, 2010. He claimed they last spoke the morning of March 23rd, but cell-phone records show they communicated throughout the day. Toha provided the Coral Springs Police a translated letter from Surya that claimed she was unable to live with herself after being raped by a coworker of her husband's at the Turnpike Authority. "This is a true letter," it proclaimed.

Surya's sister contacted the police from Jakarta and told them that Toha's claims of a happy marriage were false. Her sister, she said, urged her not to come for a visit, because Toha was convinced his wife was having an affair and the situation was bad in their home.

Off-duty police investigators scoured Crystal Lake in their personal boats the weekend after Surya was reported missing, but could not find anything. On a hunch, they looked in the industrial park, where Toha was working as a repair tech for the turnpike authority. There, they saw a video surveillance camera pointed at the lake and a hole in the fence surrounding the industrial park. The day of the press conference, police divers pulled Surya's body from the lake. It had been placed in the passenger compartment of her 2001 Daewoo Nubira. Her head was covered with a plastic bag. She had been killed by blunt force trauma to the head and then suffocated as she was dying from her injuries.

Munawar was taken into custody the day after Surya's remains were recovered. Three months after his arrest, he was arraigned on additional charges of trying to hire a hit man to kill four prosecution witnesses and dispose of their remains in the Everglades. The couple's two boys, who were 5 and 9 at the time of their mother's murder, are now in the custody of a maternal aunt. Their father remains incarcerated in a Broward County jail, awaiting trial.

After he was arrested, the Coral Springs Police released the surveillance footage from the night Surya was dumped in the lake. It shows a man who looks like Toha pulling up to the fence line with his wife's car and removing his bicycle from the trunk. He fumbles in the trunk for several minutes, as though he is checking to make sure he has not forgotten anything. He climbs into the driver's seat, and drives through the fence. Then he gets out of the car and tries to push it over an embankment into the lake. When he cannot, he climbs back into the car and drives it into the water. The car sinks into the lake and drifts. Moments later, the man runs back up the bank, shining a flashlight. He drives his bicycle away, never looking back. In all, it took only 6 minutes and 48 seconds to dump her body and leave the scene. The lights from the car are still shining eerily as the man pedals away.

There are no markers at the site where Surya entered the lake. There are no markers to show where any of the people have died here. The industrial park is lined with cold concrete and pink oleander bushes, the same color as the lipstick Surya wore in her passport photo. Their fragrant blossoms won't tell you a woman was dumped here—unless you know how to listen to them.

My ears have always been keen to danger. One day, not long after Toha was arrested, when I was home alone, I heard a woman screaming for help. I grabbed my phone and ran for the front door. In the parking lot, I saw a man attacking a woman. I had seen him out there months before, in handcuffs. The arresting policemen had emptied his pockets and laid out a bag of crack and a pipe across the hood of their cruiser. Now, he had a woman by the throat and was slamming her head into the side of a black SUV. He was bigger than the woman, and stronger, and I was three floors above them. The only thing I had was my voice. I began screaming as I dialed 911, screaming to the woman that it was going to be all right, that help was on the way. I continued to scream on the phone with the dispatcher, so the woman would hear me, so she would know that someone was watching, that someone had not lost sight of her. I screamed at the man as I gave the address to the dispatcher, I screamed out his description, and I told him to let her go, that the police were coming.

"Could you please stop screaming?" asked the dispatcher calmly.

"No," I screamed back at her, "I really can't." And I didn't. I couldn't. The voice didn't feel like it was coming from me. I am not a screamer. My normal reaction would have been to call 911 from behind a locked door and hope for the best rather than announce my presence to a violent crackhead. That day was different. I continued to scream until the man let the woman go and another neighbor took her into his apartment to wait for the police.

The narrow strip of fabric holding us to life is always as thin as my sister's dress the day my stepfather hung her out that car window. In an instant, the seams unravel, the duck comes flying at your head, your heart stops beating, the apartment catches fire, your brain explodes an aneurysm. No matter how safe we fool ourselves into believing we are, we are all dangling over some highway, held by a hand whose grip is remarkably unreliable.

Crystal Lake is not an evil place. It is no different than any other neighborhood in America in its tendency to twist toward violence. If there is evil, then it is not isolated to the upper branches of an oak tree on Crystal Lake. If there is a devil, then he wears an ordinary face. He is the man in the parking lot, taking the chance that the woman he is beating has a skull strong enough not to shatter against the steel frame of an SUV. He is the man begging for help to locate the wife whose body he has already hidden, crying for the children whose mother he has already murdered.

What is different for me now is that, in my own home, I can view the violence as separate from my daily routine. Inside these walls, I am building a safe place that is insulated from the madness. I am thankful that in three years, the only fight I have had with Matt has been over whether or not to purchase a washer and dryer for the apartment—and I know that eventually he will give in. If I have gained anything by moving to Crystal Lake, it is a solid door that locks to a world I am finding increasingly difficult to observe in silence.

Miami Redux

Corey Ginsberg

Third Coast, 2013

> To spend time in Miami is to acquire
> a certain fluency in cognitive dissonance.
>
> JOAN DIDION, MIAMI

19.

The gun is under the mattress in my roommate Kacee's bedroom. I know it's there because I asked her where it was before she left for her meeting across town.

The idea of having a gun isn't something I ever thought I'd be comfortable with, let alone happy about. Three years of living in my house in North Miami, and six years total in South Florida, has changed me in a lot of ways. The change is unavoidable. All of a sudden here I am, asking for the location of the gun, hoping—but not quite believing—that if it comes down to it, the trigger finger won't disappoint.

The gun has been the essential, uncomfortable thing that's rarely mentioned and seldom seen. It's what Kacee brings out of her room at 4:00 a.m. when the alarm goes off and the back door's kicked in. It's the hand ornament she totes on the front porch when the neighbors have a domestic disturbance on their stoop and the guy across the street with the tattooed neck threatens his girlfriend, the "stupid bitch."

I want the neighbors to know we've got a gun here. That the one they keep robbing—the vulnerable girl in the corner lot—she will fight back. I want them to be as afraid of me as I've become of them.

The house is silent, still. I look out the living room window. Cops have swarmed my neighbor's house—the corner lot across from mine. Two in bullet-proof vests peer in the windows of the small white car in her side yard, a car that intermittently appears and disappears from her property though no one seems to ever drive. Two other officers search along the perimeter of her house, stopping to glance through the barred windows. I try not to rustle the curtains I'm hiding behind as I sneak looks.

An hour passes, then another. It's hard to spend the afternoon writing with the scene out there. Two large SUVs with tinted windows come by; they drop off men in dark shirts who stand looking perplexed. Another hour passes. It's Friday, my day off, and I want to go for a run before the heat wins. But whomever or whatever the men are searching for seems to be missing, perhaps still on the loose.

I call the Miami-Dade Police Department, tell them my address, and describe what I can glean of what's going on. "I just want to make sure it's safe to go for a run," I say. "I don't want to get shot."

"Regarding this incident, it seems to be resolved," the woman on the phone says. There's a long hesitation on the other end. "I mean, I can't promise you won't get shot while running, though."

After I hang up, I imagine Kacee's gun in my hands, feel the heft of destruction resting between my trigger finger and palm. I can almost hear the sharp crack of finality, smell the gunpowder lingering on the tips of the air after I release a round. I imagine the bullet in freeze-frames as it travels toward its flesh target, slowing down incrementally like Zeno's Paradox of the Arrow.

I imagine being in charge of the situation. Being indestructible. I imagine my home is my fortress, and nothing could ever take it from me.

18.

People are calling him the Miami Zombie. Rudy Eugene, 31, was shot four times, and ultimately killed, before he ended his bloody attack on a homeless man. It happened last week on the MacArthur Causeway, less than 10 miles from my house. The assault went on for 18 minutes, and left the majority of Ronald Poppo's face chewed off, including his eye, lip, and most of his ear.

Eugene's girlfriend, who prefers to remain anonymous, shares her take on Eugene's behavior: "He loved God. He always read the Bible. Everywhere he went his Bible went." She has suspicions, though. She suspects he was drugged, that he was out of control of his actions. She suspects a Vodou curse, despite her boyfriend having no ties to the practice other than being Haitian.

What the news and its surrounding dialogue seem to notice less than the terrible specifics, though, is that Eugene had been arrested eight times since he was 16. He was the first person tasered by North Miami Beach Police during a 2004 battery incident, in which he told his mother, "I'll put a gun to your head and kill you," then threatened an officer.

"Thank God you're here," Ruth Eugene had told the responding cop. "He would have killed me."

She now believes, however, that the policeman, who shot multiple bullets into Eugene—the first several of which did nothing to deter his attack—could have used a taser gun. Just like eight years ago. "He gave me a nice card on Mother's Day," she points out. "Everybody says that he was a zombie, but I know he's not a zombie; he's my son."

Even for a city overflowing with the unexpected and inexplicable, Eugene's actions have jarred people here in a way that little else does, including Heat games and natural disasters. Although the people in Miami have grown desensitized to so much of the filler violence each day brings, this crime resonates at an octave that everyone hears but can't quite translate. It's a different pitch of uncertainty. It transformed even the simplest of actions—walking across a causeway in daylight—into worry.

The Miami I know has constructed stories about Eugene. Rather than dealing with the possibility that at least to some extent this man was a by-product of his environment, our gym and checkout-line discourse has collapsed into a plague of theories, into ways of understanding the action isolated from the actor. Zombie apocalypse. LSD delirium. Bath salts. A heat-induced violent break. We construct tales because sometimes the context isn't apparent. Or wanted. We form stories because the Why eludes, entices. Because fiction is easier than reality.

17.

I'm midsentence typing when the first boom explodes. It has that nebulous quality of evading direction and therefore being impossible to pinpoint. The dogs scatter. I run to the newly painted front window in the family room.

I'm tired of trying to decipher the Morse code of eruptions in my neighborhood. Is it a gun? Has their meth lab exploded? Is it some stupid punk setting off fireworks at 1:15 p.m. on a Saturday? I never know how worried I should be.

There's a commotion on my street, a few houses to the left—where the family lives whose dogs got loose two years ago and attacked my dachshund while we were walking. The family who lied to my face and insisted their dogs weren't to blame, and refused to pay the $1,000 vet bill Joey's 40 stitches and punctured stomach required. A black, windowless van is parked in their front yard, and three men in black vests that say POLICE on the back in block letters stand in the street staring at the house. One is behind a body-length shield. They look ridiculously out of place against the quiet suburban backdrop.

I intermittently watch the scene unfold, stepping away from my writing and into the front yard every 15 minutes or so to take inventory of what's going on. Not that it does any good. Although the number of cops changes every time I come out, no progress seems to be happening. Between two and five puzzled-looking men linger. They glance over at me but don't seem interested in filling me in. Again I'm left trying to arrange the pieces.

I imagine a hostage situation, imagine the man who lied to me has shot his wife and has his two children held at gunpoint. Or maybe someone's broken in and is demanding ransom. It could be a bomb scare and everyone on my block is in danger. Maybe they're all hiding behind their nearly identical front windows in their nearly identical one-story houses.

Imagination gets me only so far, though. Then it's back to the same ambiguous weekend scene, the confusing reality of the moment and its trickle of unknown potentials. I don't know what else to do, so I sit down in front of my computer and go back to writing.

16.

It's *not* a bad neighborhood.
It's not a *bad* neighborhood.
It's not a bad neighborhood.
It's where my house is.
It's home.

15.

The short man with choppy English who lives across the street wanders into my yard while I'm watering flowers. He hasn't talked to me in the two-plus years I've been in the neighborhood. Instead of introducing himself, he hands me a flimsy business card.

"Hey. Hey, um okay, I need to know who built your fence," he says before I can read his name.

I point the hose away from the patch of lawn he's standing on. The fence has been up for two years, so it's odd that he's only now interested in it. Something else must have happened in the neighborhood to spur his visit. I introduce myself and extend a hand to shake, a gesture he quickly and uninterestedly returns.

"Everyone on street—robbed," he says, pacing. He raises his tan hand and lifts two fingers. He makes sure I understand.

"I was robbed twice, too," I offer, but he's not interested in my story; he waves his hand before I can explain.

"They's fuckers. Son-of-a-bitch. They come through bathroom window. I go after them and try to cut them with machete." He makes a slicing motion with his stubby arm, a vision I immediately wish to purge from my memory. "But they gone out back and over fence with my boy's computer."

After 15 minutes of his diatribe, I turn off the hose and go inside to get the contact information of the contractor who built my fence. I hope this will signal that our conversation is over, but my neighbor's not done. Most of the stories he recounts I know bits of from Joanne, the woman down the street in the tan house with the basketball hoop. Two men in black ski masks tried to break down her storm door last summer while her grade-school sons were home and she was at the store. But other snippets, such as that the current robbery streak has involved complete stripping of the houses—tens of thousands of dollars of flat-screen televisions, appliances, and whatever else can be quickly lifted—is news to me.

As we're talking, a thin, wiry-looking woman staggers down the road, pausing to glare at us before moving on down the street to another neighbor's trash can. She lifts the lid and peeks in, then turns back at us as if she's found some treasure and doesn't want us to know it's there.

"She spy," my neighbor insists. "They send spy first, then come rob when not home."

The man has worked himself up into a compact ball of rage and digs his sandals into my grass. Every burglary story he recounts takes him closer to what I hope is the pinnacle of his rambling. But just like I feel when I tell people about being robbed—that vulnerable, intrusive insecurity I struggle with for months after each break-in—talking about it only makes the reality worse.

How do I know that his son—the tattooed, pierced girlfriend-berater who's always smoking pot on the front porch with his pack of sketchy friends—isn't the one robbing me? How can I be sure that this man's not here to scout out my points of entry and deliver the information to his kid? How can I trust anyone when everyone's a suspect?

"We gonna move when market better," my neighbor says. The way he stares at me implies maybe I've thought the same. I have. But as I look back at my home, I feel proud of its transformation. You don't abandon something just because it's broken. Or because things are hard. You fight harder for what you love.

14.

The article in the *Miami Herald* explains what the commotion was last night while we were grilling. Just down the road from my house, at the Funeraria Latina funeral home, 14 persons were shot, and two killed, in what the *Herald* calls: "one of the bloodiest public shootings in recent South Florida history."

The article mentions that the perpetrator is still loose, that the helicopter search was to find him before he left the North Miami area. This explains the sound in the sky my dinner guests and I felt—the undulating, wobbling drone, with the corresponding vibration our bodies registered while sipping drinks and turning vegetable skewers. It explains the copter that ducked down on my block, shining its quick figure-eight swoop on my borders before moving on to grace my neighbors with the light show. This explains the symphony of sirens that faded into an encore of ambulances and honking.

The article says that members of several South Florida gangs were at the wake, paying their respects to 21-year-old Morvin Andre. A member of one gang reached into Andre's casket to touch the body, and this spurred other gang members to open fire. The dispute that began inside poured out into the parking lot, where a gang member retrieved a handgun and assault rifle from his car. Crossfire ensued. A 5-year-old was shot.

I pass this funeral home often on my weekend runs. I study the parked hearses, the solemn-looking men holding the hands of women in black hats and sensible dresses. I round the corner toward the library where I work, next to the Biscayne Bay. About a mile down the road is the blue swatch of water I head to on my lunch break to meditate, a place so apart from the rest of Miami it feels like a mirage inside an urban jungle.

There are countless tragedies blossoming from the headlines in the newspaper and spilling onto the sidewalk over which I run and the asphalt on which I drive. To try to make sense of them leaves the brain struggling, piece-by-piece, to construct some sort of coherent, believable narrative.

13.

It's Friday night, and I'm on my way to a writing workshop on campus, three miles from my house. I watch as the lines of traffic—backed up in all six directions—get longer, as more cars pile behind the ones at the light. Something's going on and it's going to make me late. When the car in front of me crawls around the bend at the intersection, I'm first in line. That's when I glance down. There's a woman lying in the street. At first her body looks like a bent piece of metal, like garbage.

A man sits in the road next to her, rocking a small, crying girl. He seems panicked; he shields her head with his palm. The child looks up and peers in through my windshield. Our eyes meet. Her expression asks something of me. Then she glances back at the woman on the pavement. She cries louder, her pigtails bobbing. The man rocks her faster.

We're at a busy intersection on Dixie Highway. It's rush hour on Friday. At any moment the unavoidable round of honking will begin.

I want to get out of my car and throw myself in front of the little girl. Plug her ears. Protect her from their horns, their eventual tearing out in rage, the coming onslaught of middle-finger gestures. I want to shield her from the Miami I know, from what awaits her once the woman, who may well be her mother, is peeled off the road. But I don't. From inside my car I realize I'm not sure which team I'm on. So often I'm the one honking, swearing, bloated with impatience. Instead of helping I inch forward around the bend, conforming to the pulse of traffic. My Volkswagen crawls onward. The dead woman is less than 5 feet from my front left tire.

In the classroom 10 minutes later, I turn to my friend, whose truck I noticed was behind me at the accident. "Did you see the dead woman in the intersection on Dixie?" I ask Tim as we take our seats toward the back of the room.

"Yeah." He looks down. "That's the second one I've seen today."

I spend the duration of workshop trying to not remember the little girl's face. I want to forget the obtuse angle of the woman's body on the road. And the car just around the bend, its driver's door open but nobody inside. I offer myself placations about how little help I could have been—if I'd have tried. I tell myself a lot of things, but a story's already lodging itself between the books in my mental library.

Maybe the little girl and her mom were walking to get a Popsicle—the kind with two sticks that you break in half and share before the sweet orange river drips down your wrist. Or a Twix bar and a Slurpee. Maybe they were headed to a bus stop to go to the beach to feed seagulls crusts from last week's Wonder Bread. Maybe they had plans and that's why her daughter had on a pink outfit, the scrunchies in her hair perfectly matching her watermelon-colored shorts.

And the man: He could have been rushing home late from the office to spend time with his family before he took off for Friday Poker night. Or on his way to get a pack of hot dogs and some charcoal for the grill. Maybe he rounded that bend the same way I do when I'm on my way to work on Wednesdays: late, fuming and sloppy, with at best a partial regard for my surroundings. Maybe as he shielded the little girl—his face unwilling to bend and acknowledge the overwhelming remainder of the scene—he desperately wished that all the decisions he'd made in his life hadn't led him to that intersection, at that moment, in Miami.

12.

My mom drops hints.

"I just want you to have options," she tells me on the phone a few nights after I mention how overwhelmed I am. Another agent passed on my novel after requesting the whole manuscript. Another problem with my car. Another mishap with my paycheck at the writing center. Carpenter ants, too, on the newly built porch and in the walls of the house. Their tiny dead bodies wash out in a wave from the baseboards when the torrential rains finally succeed in making their way through the ceiling in my dining room.

She's coming dangerously close, again, to suggesting I sell my house—my burden—and consider other options. My mom offers advice like some offer babies to orphanages: couched in a fuzzy blanket but still a shrieking, unwanted insistence. Maybe she hoped that after nearly two and a half years as a homeowner my luck would have turned.

"Don't you remember how hard it was for me to move here? To leave Pittsburgh and start over?" My voice teeters the way it sometimes does when I try to balance my preconceived promise I won't get emotional with my mounting need for release. She's forgetting how miserable I was up north, once my friends had moved away and I was a deserted island. When I vent about Miami she doesn't remember the day I got the call that I got into the writing program at FIU, how I had to pull over to the shoulder of the highway because I was crying happy tears and almost crashed my car. "I'm not leaving my friends, my writing groups, my job," I tell her. "Where would I go?"

"You could still live in Miami, just a different neighborhood. Maybe a different street. Even an apartment."

This, I know, is a concession. My mom dislikes Miami because she defines it by its August hell-heat, its frenetic post offices, frenzied airports, and erratic drivers. Through me she knows its litany of break-in stories, its robbery streak each summer when school lets out, and its unresponsive, apathetic police officers. She internalizes and echoes the swatches of the story I so readily give when I'm upset. My mom has, of course, constructed Miami in the same way I interpret events—by the snippets I'm exposed to. She made a quilt of mismatched fabric patterns I've been hoarding and selectively doling out.

Only I don't want advice. I ask only for her to listen. What I've got—this city I've chosen, this scurvy house and lifestyle I've cultivated—it's not a matter of "fixing" it, it's a matter of understanding and being prepared. Despite everything, I like it here. Despite everything, Miami has become my home. And, just like the once-decrepit house my parents bought and transformed into their home in Pittsburgh, I revel in my house's metamorphosis.

My parents are stakeholders. They invested in the property, loaned me the money for the down payment, which is the only reason I won the bidding war. My mom was the one who ordered me a washer and dryer after going with me to the Laundromat on Dixie Highway during her first visit, who insisted I never go back to that pervert den, where eyes hung from us like suction cups and rows of men watched, mesmerized, as my bras went in soapy circles. She and my dad were the ones who bought me my 7-foot PVC fence after her second visit, when a man walked past my backyard and shouted, "Show me your cunt!" while we were in the pool. An hour later she was on the phone getting estimates from contractors to fortify my borders.

While I appreciate their generosity and concerns, there are so many parts to this story she's forgetting. When she was in town for my 30th birthday in November, she couldn't believe all the progress I'd made in such a short time. She was in awe of the new paint job I'd given the house the previous summer, the landscaping of the backyard I'd been working on incrementally. The quotes I hand-painted in the writing room along the rebuilt walls and ceiling. The tiled, screened-in porch I designed and painted. The thrift store furniture I sanded, stained, and polyurethaned so that my guests would have a place to sit at dinner parties.

"It's just that with your house . . . and your car . . . and—" my mom begins.

I know where this is going. It's going to the place so many of our fights of late go, to the avalanche zone, the dominoes match, the I-spy-with-my-little-eye what's wrong with your life (and it's everything) place that's the opposite of what I need to hear when I'm melting down. This is why our calls have collapsed into sporadic vignettes, into spoilers to a movie that isn't a memoir but is based on actual events.

"Please don't tell me to sell my house," I plead.

What I try to explain but fail to find words for is that Miami is a city of concessions. Sure, I have to wait an hour in line at the post office, but the beach is two miles away. Sure, it can be scary walking at night, but when they're in Pittsburgh shoveling a foot of snow from the driveway and scraping out their cars in the 10-degree February mornings, I'm wearing sunglasses meditating on a lawn chair, slathered in tanning oil. Sure, there's an epidemic of perpetual traffic, but I pick my hours at work to avoid the bulk of it.

What I want to tell my mom is that Miami seduces you with its dichotomies. It pulls you in with its palm trees, its pastel building palate, and promise of outdoor concerts in January. It lures you with its beautiful bait, its sandy sanctuary. Miami infects you, infuses you. You take on its arrhythmia, shoulder its promiscuity, then turn the other way when external voices question its legitimacy.

I'm defensive of Miami in the same way one defends a dysfunctional relationship. It's one thing to criticize Miami, it's another to criticize someone's choice to stay who knows its flaws and blemishes from so many angles. Living here, you grow used to the choppy waves. You stay afloat by not drowning. You tell yourself it's worth it—and it is. But the moment you let down your guard and forget to fight the undertow, the rip current wins.

"Corey, you're not listening to me."

"I have to go now," my voice squeaks before I hang up.

11.

It's dark in the house. Hot, too. The air inside feels wrong, like it's been trapped in an attic and abandoned. I'm not allowed to call FPL to restore the power until the cops pull prints from every surface and from the power box outside my window, with the wires cut like open veins.

Kacee and I sit in the driveway in her car, blasting the air-conditioning. Neither of us speaks. What is there to say? Even though I'd told her about the robbery last summer before she moved in and warned her there's always a chance it could happen again if she decided to rent a room, how could she suspect her laptop would be the next one stolen?

It's not sadness I feel as I sit there. It's more like a self-imposed vacuum. My only thought as I wait for the cops to arrive is how long I can keep this façade going. I did everything right this time. Bought the alarm system. Set it. Had Kacee bring her big dog from Texas. Told her it was okay to have her gun. Still my house was targeted. It's been two years of this struggle and I don't know when things are going to change. Or if they will. How long and hard can I fight for Miami, for my home?

10.

The North Miami Beach Sexual Offender list is mailed out several times a year. From its thin pages stare out the mug shots of dozens of tired-looking men, and every once in a while a wild-eyed woman.

The first year I lived in my house I forced myself to read it in its entirety, noting the addresses of the listings, calculating their proximity to my house. For a while I scoped the houses on my morning runs, pairing the men who shouted offensive slurs at me to their paper profiles. I stopped running down the street parallel to mine. *Maybe if I can control this one variable I'll be safe*, I thought.

My house still got robbed. So did my car. I couldn't stop the inevitable.

When the list arrives today, almost two years after I bought my house, I glance at it for a long moment, straddling the awkward in-between of the idioms "Knowledge is power" and "Ignorance is bliss." For once I fall into the gray zone, a realm I'm never comfortable treading in. I throw the mailer away.

What good, I wonder, are the facts, when they do nothing to alter the situation? What good is it to know that in North Miami we have one registered sex offender for every 1,650 residents? While this is half as many as the state average, and is much less than Miami Gardens' one sexual offender per 37 residents, what good can possibly come from me knowing the truth?

No matter which direction I run in, if I go down enough streets in my neighborhood I'm statistically likely to pass at least a few of these houses. How hard would it be to follow me home and watch me go in my front door? To pass on word that the woman who just finished putting the last coat of paint on her house likes to run before work in the morning? To note my schedule, car, and pattern, and pencil it in between the other North Miami day raids? No matter how many facts, switchblades, or escape plans I arm myself with, there's no real way to ultimately be prepared for what may follow me home.

9.

Home. Home is a mat at the front door that's dirty from tread, but not dirty enough to throw away just yet. It's knowing where the mismatch set of dishes go and where the car keys hide. It's a potted herb garden on the porch, a rusted fire pit in the back next to the perpetually kinked hose, naked of nozzle. Home is a couch that doesn't poke in a room that isn't painted white. It's a cracked driveway with enough room for a geriatric, semi-reliable car. It's waving to the man at the end of the street who's always watering his yellow lawn. Home is a wine rack with at least one bottle and a refrigerator stocked with cheese—just in case. Home is handing out candy and juice boxes on Halloween and putting up the Christmas tree the next day. Home is not three-month sublet, bitchy landlord, or loud, sex-having neighbors, one wall removed. Home isn't entrapment. It's not regret. It's mine, not theirs. Home is full-length memoir instead of collection of essays.

8.

"You know there's a bunch of jewelry and foreign money on your roof, right?" the plumber says as I pace the hallway at work on my cell phone between tutoring sessions with students.

It's months after I called the cops to tell them about the man on my roof, half a year removed from the night they blew me off.

Now that I know that someone really was there that night, recalling the officers' indifference infuriates me. I can still see the male and female cops when they came to my house. They kept me waiting for 30 minutes after my frantic 911 call.

"He's on my roof," I'd said to them when they knocked, speaking softly through the metal slits in the front door.

The officers looked as tired as I felt. They seemed more interested in checking my eyes for pupil dilation than in exploring the sounds I had called about. The officers seemed to have constructed a story about me.

"I know this sounds crazy." I hoped that offering up front the seeming absurdity of calling in about what they might assume was a large raccoon would gain me pathos. I wanted them to know that I knew the difference between animals walking and human footsteps. This wasn't a raccoon.

The cops told me they didn't need to come in. They backed away from my front door, shone their flashlights at the slanted part of my roof, and shook their heads. I followed them to the side of my house, around the row of decorative grasses I'd planted and the line of cypress pines by the fence. In the backyard, they shone the light over the surface of the pool, then quickly swept the beam over the roof.

"We don't see anything," the officer said, her voice betraying a hint of accusation.

"Don't you want to go up and check it out?"

They shook their heads. "No need. If he was here he's gone now."

The officers extended me a courtesy hour in which they parked in front of my house. But when they left a few hours before sunrise, I was alone again, with my expensive alarm system programmed, its red HAL eye glaring at me as I paced the living room with my switchblade in one hand, my cell phone in the other. As I brewed a pot of strong, black coffee, I imagined him pacing 10 feet above me, our footsteps synchronizing like parallel heartbeats.

The call from the plumbers today brings back the faded mosaic of anger. When I get home from work I examine the loot the workers left, which is in a plastic Publix bag. It contains nothing of real value, just some gaudy costume bling, a few dozen unidentifiable coins, and a set of chipped, faux-silver bangles. Still, I call the cops.

"I want you to put on record that I'm not crazy," I say to the officer when he arrives.

The policeman looks up from the notes he's scribbling. He sets the pen down and takes the bag from me. His face is apologetic as I explain how my story was initially discounted, and that the female officer rolled her eyes when she thought I wasn't looking.

"When I call you guys, you need to know I'm telling the truth and really need help," I insist. "I need you to know that I'm not crying wolf."

7.

It's evident from studying my backyard on Sunday morning that the first pool party at my house was a success. As I skim the surface of the water, retrieving beer cans, red cups, stray tortilla chips, used paper plates, and disintegrating cocktail napkins, I smile through my veil of hangover at evidence of debauchery from the previous night.

Some of the guests are still in the house, passed out at various stages of drunkenness and nakedness, partially wrapped in damp towels. They crashed on couches after I went to bed at 5:00 a.m.

Last night nobody cared that the pool is green from the algae buildup resulting from the poor circulation of the pump system. It didn't matter that I have almost no furniture or that only one toilet flushes. My friends didn't notice the crumbling plaster in the living room or the dirt in the corners of the guest rooms I haven't had a chance to paint in the three months I've lived here.

All that mattered last night was that there was cold beer, dirty vodka, layered bean dip, and a pool with a big raft. For those few wonderful hours, it was easy to forget about the rest of Miami and imagine that my house was an island to itself.

6.

The sound the new ADT alarm system makes is relentless. A constant, high-pitched moan that cuts through the hum of the newly installed central air system. It helps me remember, every second, that I'm paying $50 a month to be on lockdown in my house. So do the stickers and signs posted on the front and back windows, on the side of the house and in the lawn.

If I *really* want to feel safe, I was told, I should put bars on my windows. That's the only sure way to keep in, in, and to keep out, out.

No matter how hard I tried, I couldn't imagine myself staring out my front windows from behind metal pinstripes. Choosing, even facilitating, imprisonment is the opposite of feeling at home. It's not something I'm okay with. It's not something I'll ever be okay with.

5.

I unlock the front door. Joey runs up to me, pawing at my legs, panting in the thick living-room heat. I set my backpack on the couch. The thermostat reads 89, and I wonder how deep into a Miami summer I can make it without AC. It hasn't even been two months in the house, and the sticky hot is starting to wear on me.

I don't notice my laptop is gone until I sit on my bed, where I left the computer before work. When I go to check my e-mail I realize it's not on the pillow and isn't plugged into the phone jack. It hits me, then, that I've been robbed.

I run into the kitchen, grab a butcher knife and the dog, and call 911 from the front porch. As I wait for the police, I stare at the groupings of newly planted flowers lining the walkway, their pink heads wilted from the heft of July heat.

When the officer arrives he scours my house for signs of the intruder, but whoever took my laptop, camera, and iPod is gone.

"They usually watch you for a few weeks," he tells me as he examines my living room. "They like to slip in through a window in the back—then do a clean sweep."

The cost of replacing my stolen property: $2,475. My homeowner's deductible: $2,500. What's worse than the devastating monetary loss, though, is that the e-mail I sent this morning containing my novel outline didn't go through because of poor Internet connection. The backbone to my book is gone.

I imagine the person who stole my computer going through my files, deleting the hundreds of poems, folders full of fiction, and my collection of essays that was my master's thesis I defended only months ago. I envision him dumping my novel outline into the little trashcan at the top left of my desktop. Maybe he makes a clean sweep of the hard drive before he sells my Inspiron to the nearest pawnshop on Dixie Highway, the one next to my Laundromat. Maybe he buys a gun with the money they give him. Maybe he'll rob me again, now that he knows his way into my bed.

4.

"You're not Bob Vila," my friend tells me. "You're a writer."

Michael is right; in the weeks since I bought the house I haven't had time to devote to much of anything creative. Between installing a new electrical system, a new hot water heater, new locks, a new garage door, and a new sink, and spending my nights mopping up after the periodic living room floods during June, every shred of downtime has been consumed thus far. The house has become my newest art project; its rapid evolution is staggering, not just to the neighbors who compliment the front yard, but to me as well. Every small change pays off big, like sanding and painting the front door, tearing out the weeds that blocked the front windows, and arranging solar lights to illuminate my front pathway.

But I can't just set my writing aside. The house won't be done in a few months, or a few years, and I have to carve out time for what's important. Besides, things are looking good. The guest room's painted, and I've refinished some furniture so no room is completely bare.

I sit on my couch and tell myself I won't get up until I have an idea for a novel. The long form in writing is something that's always terrified me, and I hate letting my fear limit my output. I stare at the painting over my TV—a lake surrounded by pine trees. Its dark backdrop looks ominous, like a storm's approaching. For an hour I let the image dance in my skull and mingle with the other bits bunking there. Ideas begin to stick to one another. Thoughts expand. I jot notes as quickly as I can type while pieces of a potential book gallop head-on at me. When I finish transcribing, I realize I've done something I've never been able to do—outline a large project, completely, chapter by chapter.

I save the file, but the Internet is down so I'll have to wait till the morning to e-mail it to myself.

3.

Rain patters against the roof as I sit on the couch meditating before work. Joey's curled into a tight nugget in my lap, despite the lack of air-conditioning and the 90-degree heat. Just as I relax enough to allow in the floating sensation that corresponds with deep release, Joey begins a round of crazed barks and lunges onto the floor. Before my eyes adjust to the light I know something's wrong.

The dog races to the double French doors that lead into my backyard, barking at a man in a yellow raincoat who stares in through the glass with a cupped hand. My body reacts, though my mind has yet to translate. I run to the kitchen and grab a knife. It's not till I'm at the door that I realize I'm screaming.

"What the fuck are you doing in my yard?" I pound the butt of my free hand against the pane of glass closest to the tall man's face.

Despite the blur of action on my end, he remains conspicuously calm. The man takes a step back and slowly answers, "Hey, we're cool, we're cool. I'm homeless—just wanted to stay dry." Raindrops fall from the folds of his slicker as he shows me his palms.

"This is my house!" I scream.

The man makes no attempt to leave. He mumbles, "I thought it was still empty."

I study the lawn furniture on the back porch, the rafts floating in the pool, the shrubs I've planted over the past month, and the newly edged and mowed lawn. "Get the fuck off my property," I insist over Joey's barks.

The man turns and shuffles toward my front yard and the street.

My hands are shaking so violently I have a hard time checking the locks on the back doors. I know I should call 911, but I'm already late for work and will have students waiting for tutoring help at the writing center. I need the money and can't risk getting fired or losing half a day of wages at a job I just started. I step into the front yard and watch the man go farther and farther from my house, the tail end of his raincoat hitting his hiking boots as he fades into the hazy morning.

I think back to the sound of walking on my back porch I sometimes hear at night, to the smell of urine on the side of my house, to the empty beer bottles in brown paper bags strewn on my lawn and the midnight rustling of hedges between my yard and my neighbors'. What if none of it has been my imagination? What if the mental dichotomy I draw in my brain between dream delirium and waking life has allowed the reality of what's going on to remain hidden in the shadows?

2.

"You shouldn't be running here," the policeman says to me, peering through the sliver in his tinted window at my sweat-soaked body next to his car.

It's noon on a Saturday. I'm not sure what I've done wrong. I take out a headphone bud and point to the street behind me. "But I live here," I say, studying the cluster of purple flowers in the front yard of the woman down the street. "This is my neighborhood."

The officer nods a solitary nod—a nod of lost causes—and even behind sunglasses I can sense his preemptive *I-told-you-so* expression. His eyes linger on me for a long moment before he rolls up his window and drives onward.

The sun glares at me. Watching, always watching, as I continue running.

1.

"You don't want to live in a neighborhood where people have fences in their front yards," Diana assures me as she pulls into the driveway of the last house we're going to see that day.

The only thing I find more infuriating than someone telling me how to feel is them projecting their wants onto me. Diana knows me as well as she knows how to drive her Lexus while talking on her cell phone and sipping a Starbucks venti macchiato. If she had any understanding of my wants, she wouldn't have left me sitting in a parking lot in Fort Lauderdale outside her realty office this morning—Easter—for an hour. If Diana were listening to me, she'd have been taking me to the houses I've asked to see, not to gated communities in Boca Raton and Palm Beach with HOA costs higher than the monthly salary I'll be making as a tutor. Had she heard a word I said this past month, she'd have avoided the other end of the spectrum, too: crumbling investments in lots full of garbage next to the Walmart and Dollar Store. Depraved neighborhoods that skirt the threshold between avoided and abandoned—the kind you double-check to make sure your car windows are up and your doors are locked when you drive through.

This neighborhood isn't like the others. People are walking their dogs. Trees line the block. Families are outside playing music, grilling, and washing cars.

We pull up the street of the last house I've asked to see for the day, the property just a few blocks from the apartment I've lived in for the past three years. The photos posted online look almost too good to believe its listing price. Four bedrooms. 30,000-gallon swimming pool. A garage and driveway. Palm and mango trees in the huge backyard. A front stoop and an enclosed wooden porch. A corner lot separated from the rest of North Miami by a ficus row and chain-link fence.

Diana has conveniently forgotten the keys, but I circle the house and peer in through the blinds while she sits in the air-conditioned car, talking on her phone. The inside is bigger than the photos implied. So is the yard. With each glimpse my excitement expands. Looking at that house makes everything inside of me feel right. I get chills. My skin knows. I know.

This house will be my home.

As I walk back to Diana's car, I imagine myself living here. I see myself cooking eggplant parmesan in the tile-countered kitchen, feeding it to dinner guests in the expansive living room. I see my dachshund running in the backyard, chasing lizards he'll never catch. I know how happy I'd be in a neighborhood where people smile and wave when I drive by, in a sliver of Miami where the rest of the nonsense is muted by the sound of my skillet sizzling and friends splashing in the pool. I envision myself writing on the wooden porch off the master bedroom, sipping strong, sweet coffee, imagining a world so dynamic and perplexing no narrative could do it proper justice.

Daughters of the Springs

Lauren Groff

Oxford American, 2014

A few miles southwest of Gainesville, the arching oaks of central Florida loosen into long fields full of beef steer. They tighten up again into the Goethe State Forest (pronounced, hereabouts, as Go-thee), and finally peter out into US-19, a soulless and endless miracle mile of corporate chains from Applebee's to Zaxby's, hitting nearly every letter between. In the town of Homosassa, I saw a smiling gray manatee the size of a VW van on the side of the road, surrounded by a sea of yard-sign valentines that someone had left to fade in the March sun. Homosassa is famous for being one of the best places in Florida to view West Indian manatees, those gentle thousand-pound sea cows that are routinely torn up by Jet Skis and motorboats. Skeptics believe that sailors mistook sea mammals like manatees and dugongs for women, giving rise to the myth of the mermaid. After a few months at sea, one starts to see what one expects to see, and long ago, sirens were a matter of fact, not myth. Henry Hudson reported a sighting of a mermaid and Christopher Columbus saw a manatee surfacing somewhere near the Dominican Republic on January 9, 1493, and noted in his diary that mermaids were not nearly as beautiful as they were painted. True. Manatees are pewter-colored and have faintly hound-doggish heads and platters for fins; they don't look much like Daryl Hannah. Still, the word manatee comes from the Taíno word for "breast," and a manatee on her back, with her forefins folded on her chest, can appear to have a goodly bosom. It's not hard to see how, after months of male company, the sight of one rising from the waves like a massive and fleshy woman could evoke intense erotic yearnings.

Mermaids—which I'm using here as shorthand for uncanny female water spirits—are common wherever human beings rub up against bodies of water. In Japan, there are *ningyo*, strange woman-faced semi-immortal fish figures; in ancient Syria, the goddess Derceto was described by Diodorus Siculus in his *Bibliotheca historica* as having a fishtail. There are *margyr* in Scandinavia and *sabawaelnu* in the Mi'kmaq culture of North America. There are Celtic *morgens*, aboriginal Australian *yawkyawks*, Russian *rusalki*. The Greeks had whole taxonomies of water spirits, from the Oceanids of the salt water and the Nereids of the Mediterranean to the Naiads, the spirits of fresh water. The most famous mermaids in myth— Odysseus's singing sirens whom he resisted by stoppering his sailors' ears with wax and tying himself to the mast—were not mermaids at all, but immortal bird-women, with wings, who once sang against the Muses in a competition (they lost and in punishment were plucked). That these creatures have slid from avian to piscine over the years speaks to the sexual appeal of mermaids. The sirens call men with their voices and bodies, water is voluptuous, and there's nothing sexy about a woman with a chicken's netherparts.

I think the widespread ubiquity of these dangerous, capricious female figures has less to do with lust and mistaken sea creatures than with a stunning human capacity for metaphor. Water is necessary, urgent, everywhere; it gives rise to life. It is also perilous, subject to its own laws, and contains dark and hidden depths. The makers of myths are the victors, the ones allowed the leisure and education to write (men, in other words, for most of human history). The myth of mermaids both explains and distances woman, that great and confounding mystery. And the appeal isn't just for men; girls are drawn to mermaids' wildness and beauty and power. After all, the sea creatures are the ones who get to decide if people who fall overboard will swim or sink.

I grew up as a very serious competitive swimmer on a boys' swim team and dreamed at night of being a mermaid, of flying in water and breathing as if it were air, and of luxuriating among the sea grasses and seeing the boats pass overhead like clouds over the sun. There was something about mermaids' ferocity, their danger, their uncompromising strangeness and power, that spoke to a truth deep in me. Every once in a while, even decades later, I still hear an echo of their song and feel compelled to listen.

During my drive to Weeki Wachee, I held the Starbucks siren hot in my hand. The coffee company's logo is a smirker. (I'll cop to my dislike.) She's bi-caudal and holds her split tail beside her head with both fists in a frankly pornographic manner, teasing us with the answer to the age-old mystery of how all those seamen and fish-bottomed women were physiologically able to get it on.

No matter; I was on the hunt for far better mermaids, for high-grade Americana. Weeki Wachee is one of many natural springs that run through the state of Florida. They are its best-kept secret: people think of swamp-land when they think of Florida, or oranges or theme parks or skittery dance music in some Miami nightclub—not cold, clear rivers on which you can float for miles and never come across a single alligator. From under-water, Weeki Wachee appears to be a cragged mountainside, astonishingly steep. Once the site of Timucua, or aboriginal, burial grounds, it served as a swimming and laundry pool for locals in the 1930s and early 1940s as well as their trash heap.

Walton Hall Smith was a writer (co-authoring a book titled *Liquor, Servant of Man*) and founder of the Syfo beverage company, and he had long dreamed of developing Weeki Wachee into an underground theater. In June 1946, he paired up with Newt Perry, who was famous for wrestling alligators at Silver Springs, training Navy Seals, and pioneering the un-derwater film industry in Florida; Grantland Rice called him "The Human Fish." With a group of investors, they purchased the site from the City of St. Petersburg and began constructing the theater sunk deep into the side of the springs.

The park was first opened to the public on October 12, 1947. The theater was a low building with twinned ramps that led underground, where a curved auditorium looked out into the springs from sixteen feet below the surface, so that one could see much of the chasm and all attendant wildlife: turtles, ducks, alligators, and sometimes even a stray manatee. By the time of the opening, Perry had come up with the idea of bringing in young women in bathing suits to do an underwater ballet for the tourists.

In the beginning, the Weeki Wachee mermaids were local teenagers, paid in hot dogs and hamburgers and bathing suits. There were so few cars on Route 19 that every time they heard one coming, the mermaids scampered to the side of the road to lure the drivers in for a show. How startling it must have been to be driving along the scrubby brown fields in the bright and sleepy sunlight, and then, out of nowhere, a line of young beauties in bathing suits. I wonder if anyone resisted them.

At last, Weeki Wachee hove up on the west side of the highway, a strange repository for such an ancient and resonant myth. Even at nine in the morning on a chilly March day, the parking lot was filled with cars and buses. The park itself was half-hidden like an afterthought, low-set in the lot's northeast corner. The overall aesthetic was one of midcentury painted concrete, graced here and there with nippleless female busts. Before the entrance, there's a huge fountain, and in the middle of the fountain there's an erect pillar topped by female swimmers engaged in a move I'd come to learn is called an *adagio*. Picture one swimmer vertical, fist extended, lifting another swimmer who is arched on her back toward the surface of the water. I was a little surprised by the statue's lack of tails. It turns out tails on the Weeki Wachee mermaids didn't appear until 1962: the earliest prototype was a very heavy rubber tail made for movie star Ann Blyth in the 1948 movie *Mr. Peabody and the Mermaid*. It wasn't practical: it cost twenty thousand dollars and was nearly impossible to squeeze into. These days, park employees or the mermaids themselves make the swimming tails out of stretchy fabric, with zippers on the side. There are also posing tails, with sequins and with zippers on the back, for verisimilitude, I suppose.

John Athanason, the park's genial, ruddy public relations manager, met me at the gate. John told me he'd been an employee at Weeki Wachee during its lowest moment, before it became a state park, when the private owners neglected the place to the point where there were serious safety issues, some involving fire exits and sewage. The mermaids had to launch a campaign, Save Our Tails, to keep the park from closing down. The small park is bare-bones, though there is evidence of recent sprucing: new plantings of sago palm and bougainvillea, new paint. We walked through a clump of high-schoolers to view the springs from above. Sapphire-blue in places, the source is fairly small, the hole itself not especially impressive from our vantage and angle. It looked not unlike a pond, with a wee water park called Buccaneer Bay at its far end. John told me some fascinating information—Weeki Wachee was a first-magnitude spring directly fed from the Floridan aquifer; divers know that it goes at least 413 feet deep; 117 million gallons pump out of it every day; the current in the water is five miles per hour, the temperature a constant 74.2 degrees—but I was also distracted by the teenaged boy surreptitiously copping a feel of the tiny teenaged girl on my other side. There was a man blowing leaves off the far bank. There were indolent fish.

John led me down a ramp and into the underwater theater, a large curved space with acoustic tiles and a cement floor. It was dark and empty and smelled a little of moldering eelgrass and feet. The audience sits on battered wooden benches. There is a curtain that automatically slides up to show the strange green subaqueous world where the mermaids perform, emerging from underneath shells that flip up on the large flat stage. The distant domed airlock on the far side of the chasm looks like a 1940s dream of the future. Over everything is a layer of green-brown lyngbya algae, even though, once upon a time, Weeki Wachee water was so clear people assumed a trick—that the mermaids were suspended on wires. This is Florida. People here gleefully cake their lawns and golf courses in nitrogen, then wax nostalgic for a time when the springs weren't clouded over.

In the dim blue theater with only fish and turtles sliding by, I heard the weariness in John's voice. Surely he has answered the same inane questions over and over for years, and it must be difficult to maintain a highburn enthusiasm for a place that's equally worn-down and kitschy. Still, he seemed to regard the park and the mermaids with avuncular pride. I asked if he'd ever considered inviting in a reality television show to bring some money to Weeki Wachee. He said he's had dozens of proposals, but reality television feeds on interpersonal drama, and the mermaids are employees of the State of Florida, which is not delighted about employees' interpersonal drama being sprayed about on national television. "And girls are . . . complicated," he said knowingly. I nodded and smiled, but because I'm complicated, I winced every time John called the performers *girls*. I'm a product of the politically correct '90s. When I was a belligerent fourteen-year-old *actual* girl, with a copy of *The Second Sex* in hand, I was taught to insist on being called a woman. Some of the mermaids may be very young, true, but many are in their twenties. Some are teachers, some are mothers; all are women. We were rousted from the theater by a white-blonde woman in a track suit, whom I'd later discover is a mermaid, who came into the theater and lowered the curtains over the windows to the springs. It was almost time for the first show of the day: *Hans Christian Andersen's The Little Mermaid*.

John led me into a small room so hot I nearly fell down. This was the tube room, named for the dark 64-foot underwater pipe that the mermaids have to swim through to make their way to and from the theater. The tube room has to be boiling hot because spending half an hour in 74-degree water can make one rapidly hypothermic. The mermaids came down the spiral staircase from their dressing rooms to finish their preparations for the show. The women wore cake makeup and bikini tops, tights and bloomers. They sat at the edge of a fourteen-foot well to put on water shoes and flippers and roll their tails on over it all, then zipped the tails up the side. Dry and off, the tails were a little dingy and looked like t-shirts; when they were on, the tails looked pretty realistic, if I squinted. The mermaids chatted and answered my questions when I dared to say something, but after a while it was clear that they were being painfully polite so I let them be. Here is what I learned: Karri is a crabber on her off-days and has a one-year-old daughter. Stayce, who was playing the sea witch, is a bartender at Applebee's. Tara, who was managing the safety of the mermaids from the tube, is a chipper, very beautiful mother with the kind of wavy blonde hair you think mermaids should have. One by one, they put on face masks to see their way through the tube, which they'd take off before the performance. Then they fell into the water, took the last sip of air that wasn't going to come from a hose or air-lock, did a little half flip with their tail, and disappeared into the tube. There are air hoses every few feet, but the mere thought of having to swim down an enclosed space with no scuba equipment gave me a case of the sympathetic horripilations.

Out in the theater, the audience had arrived, as if by magic. I don't know what I was expecting of a mermaid show on a cold weekday morning in March, but the place was packed with retirees in matching visors and tiny children in mermaid costumes. I suppose I'd been afraid of being the only person in the audience. I'd felt a preemptive fear for the future of this weird place; half an hour in the park, and I was already protective of it. The voice-over was careful to be sure we knew we were about

were kids in the audience, after all. But the heart wants what the head calls unlikely.

We applauded. The lights came on. We shuffled up into the sunlight and chill air and stood like heifers at the salt lick, blinking. I ate a formerly frozen pizza at The Mermaid Galley and wondered at the albino peahens wandering around, then John brought me in to meet the mermaids while they ate lunch. I'll admit that my hands were shaking; I was meeting the mermaids of my dreams! But they were mermaids in tracksuits and wet hair, eating fried foods from fast-food joints down the miracle mile, smiling at me with mildly overdrawn patience. The prince devoured a whole pepperoni pizza by himself. On land, in sunlight, in their puffy clothes, their hair slicked to their heads, it was eerie how much the mermaids resembled a women's college rugby team after a match. On dry land, the mermaids were all very pretty, but some of their glamour had been left in the shimmering water.

I wanted to suss out the mystery of the mythical mermaids, find some of their bone-deep danger, but John wouldn't let me talk one-on-one with any of the performers. "It's not that I don't trust the girls, but . . ." he said, shrugging, fiddling with his e-cigarette. So I spoke with the lot of them. They answered my questions but did not find them very good. They sighed. They love being mermaids because it was like a sorority; they love each other and are always delighted when former mermaids come back to do shows (in John's terminology, retired mermaids graduated from "girls" to "ladies"). There was no danger, really, they said: they all looked out for one another down there. They had to go through extensive physical testing, be certified in scuba diving, and have a year's worth of training before they were allowed to perform in major roles. There were air hoses and air locks nearly everywhere in the deep; there was no real worry about running out of air. John peered at me with increasing suspicion every time I asked another question about danger, sex, or myth. In desperation, having come to the end of my questions, I asked if they believe in mermaids. There was an embarrassed silence; they looked at their food as if hoping it would speak for them. One woman threw me a bone. "I mean, I do," she said. "We kind of have to. Like, we *are* mermaids. Right?" Right.

They are mermaids. They're also extremely hardworking hourly employees of the State of Florida. The state publishes its employees' wages online; it was easy to discover that one of the senior mermaids makes thirteen dollars an hour, and none of them receives benefits. They work long days, responsible for training newer mermaids, running various mermaid camps, scrubbing the algae, which they call "scrunge," off the spring-side of the windows, making sure the theater is clean and the costumes are in order, ensuring the other performers' safety, choreographing routines, and directing the shows and in-water practices from a little podlike booth off the theater. They get to dolphin-kick and smile and make pretty shapes with their bodies underwater, but the rest of the time it's a job, and it's a job that requires freezing in icy water multiple times a day. It's far more difficult than it looks. Their magic is in making it all look easy.

I went back, face burning, to the theater where the afternoon crowd poured in. The children had been replaced by late-middle-aged tourists with sunburned shins and ball caps and bewildered looks on their faces. The next show was called *Fish Tails*. It began with a video on high-mounted televisions that showed the history of Weeki Wachee, with still photographs from the past; all very informative and clear. I believe the prince from *Hans Christian Andersen's The Little Mermaid* was the announcer for this one, but I could be wrong. There was a calypso version of *Red Red Wine*. There was an Enya song I hadn't heard since middle school, when I was going through a crystals-and-Arthurian-legends phase. Some man behind me complained about his psoriasis acting up. The curtain rose.

And there, again, was the frisson of joy: how beautiful they were, those women in the blue light with their shining tails. My disbelief suspended itself, floated off to the stained acoustic tiles overhead. The mermaids ate bananas underwater; they drank some brownish drink from a glass bottle. They showed us the human elevator move, where they can regulate how high they rise or how low they sink by how much air they take in or let out from the air hoses. A yellow-bellied slider turtle the size of a steering wheel mimicked the mermaids' ballet moves and tried to nibble on their undulating hair. The mermaids bent themselves into a circle, grasping one another's tails, and spun. They shimmied and lip-synched.

During the *Little Mermaid* show, they had lip-synched a song called "We've Got the World by the Tail." It goes:

We're not like other women
We don't have to clean an oven.
And we never will grow old,
We've got the world by the tail.

And all I could think was, well, Christ, *I* don't have to clean the oven. I resisted the song when they sang it that morning, but the old-timey feel of *Fish Tails* made me think harder about the young women in 1940s Florida who had few career options beyond marriage and low-level service jobs. How glorious it must have been to be given the chance to shake their stuff in the water and live independently and hobnob with bona fide movie stars like Johnny Weissmuller (who played Tarzan) and Esther Williams, to become celebrities *themselves*, even though they were from the middle of Podunk nowhere and had little more than beauty and youth and willingness on their side. How seductive such a life would have been; it must have threatened men unused to women living independently. It must have been infuriating to see such lissome, smiling exemplars of feminine beauty through the glass—and to be unable to touch them. The women, knowing they were watched, would have felt their own terrific power. I was falling for the history of the show, for all the many mermaids who'd swum here and made it look glamorous.

The penultimate act in *Fish Tails* was advertised as a deep-dive of about 120 feet into the mouth of the chasm. Water pours out of the spring at such a speed that one former mermaid described the dive as trying to swim up a waterfall. There used to be enormous catfish that lived down there and an eel that would threaten the mermaids when they hooked their heels into the bar that held them in place. The mermaid disappeared below the lip of the stage; the announcer cannily built suspense by describing what she was feeling as she dove deeper and deeper; at one point she sent up a breath that expanded hugely as it rose, from shower cap to bread loaf to pillowcase. Time ticked and ticked. I nearly passed out by the time she came up, grinning and waving. I'd been holding my breath with her the whole time.

And then it was the final act. A super-patriotic country song boomed loud and the mermaids wore red-white-and-blue costumes and held an American flag between them. My patriotism is manifested in finding it a privilege to pay taxes, in voting, and in turning a critical eye on my government. Nationalistic bombast makes me ill. I closed my eyes to this last part of the show until the audience erupted in roars, and we all filed out, glad to be aboveground in the sunlight again. I thanked John for his real kindness and fled.

I came to Weeki Wachee to sound the mystery of the mermaid, to find danger and sex and darkness and maybe hear my own deeps echoed back. Instead I found a polite performance and excellent work ethic and real people who do what they do out of sisterhood and love for the cold springs. This is what happens when you are given a plateful of hot Americana à la mode and expect to taste profundity; my disappointment was a result of my failure of expectations, not their show. I'd brought a bathing suit, but it sat dry at the bottom of my purse. I think I'd hoped the mermaids would recognize me as one of their own and invite me in for a swim. Oh well. I did spend a day looking at beautiful women, a spectacular way to pass the time.

As I drove back to Gainesville, I thought of the Rhinemaidens. The freshwater Weeki Wachee mermaids are closer to nixies than actual mermaids, who supposedly live in the ocean; the saltwater Gulf, the *mer* of the maids, is miles away from the springs. In Richard Wagner's *Ring* cycle, the Rhinemaidens are nixies of the river Rhine and keepers of the gold that, when seized, leads to world power. They're seductive and morally ambiguous and elusive and playful. The gold is stolen from them in the first opera of the three, and at one point later they sing angrily:

> Traulich und treu
> ist's nur in der Tiefe:
> falsch und feig
> ist, was dort oben sich freut!

According to my dictionary and my shaky memory of college German, this means: Only the deeps hold intimacy and truth; false and cowardly is the surface's rejoicing.

But the surface is often beautiful; it is often good enough. I drove home in silence, letting my brain decompress. Two weeks later, I'd spend a week at Crescent Beach on the Atlantic coast of Florida, where high school students rent condos and pack them with dozens of hormonal bodies. I'd watch these teenaged girls in their bikinis, braving the cold March wind, perhaps—probably—drunk in the middle of the day, delighting in their new, gorgeous, dangerous bodies, flirting with the boys who eyed them with shielded delight, and I'd think: Aha. *Here* be sirens. But on the drive home from Weeki Wachee, the long brown fields were tender in the early-afternoon light. The blue sky appeared out of the tunnels of water oak and palmetto scrub, the air calm and cool in these last months before the heat descends like a solid fabric. I cracked the window to let in the wind. The daughters of the air were doing one good deed to earn their souls that afternoon. Sometimes it's lovely to float on the surface of things.

Security Clearance

Linda Buckmaster

Burrow Press, 2016

"Wait here. I have to put my knives in the car to get through security," my brother Ric says.

I have just met up with my brother at the entrance to the Kennedy Space Center. I never like to wait, and I *told him* earlier we'd have to go through security. We are here for "the ultimate journey," as the website says, "where the sky isn't the limit—it's just the beginning." And if that weren't enough, we also have reservations for the special bus tour offered by the Center: "Cape Canaveral Then and Now." But before we can blast off, I have to wait for Ric to drop off his knives.

My little brother, age 56, has a slow, hobbling walk. Maybe it's from decades of carrying 70 pounds of welding equipment a quarter mile to ships in dry dock. Or maybe it's from walking the streets of Jacksonville during his junkie days. Or from a deal gone bad. Now he's carrying *knives*—plural?

I can see I'll have a bit of a wait. He and I have parked our cars at the far end of the lot. His is the black Lexus, the one he got used "for a very good interest rate," he tells me, at one of those "no credit, bad credit, no problem" places. Mine is the bland rental because I've undertaken a research trip to the Florida coast, coming down from my home in Maine to try to reconstruct a childhood of wandering the palmettos and watching rockets take off. Despite previous return visits to see family, I haven't before connected my childhood geography with the present one.

"Space Coast" Florida in the 1960s is, or was, my homeplace, and I'm trying to remember it as it was in order to write about it. A confluence of

Florida geography, the Space Race against the Soviets, and the go-go era of the larger culture launched me in ways I am still learning about. When I left home as a hippie chick in 1969, I "couldn't have cared less" about the space industry, to use a favorite expression of my father's.

My reentry, on the eve of the launch of the final Space Shuttle in 2011—widely considered the end of an era at the Cape—is a conscious return to the landmarks of those early days in which I grew up. With Ric, I've visited the East Coast Surf Museum and Ron Jon's Surf Shop, where he told me stories about the locally famous surfers in the photos, and we later cruised the docks of Port Canaveral, like teenagers sharing a joint with friends.

Our father was an engineer at the Cape in the early days of the industry, the 1950s and 1960s, and I want to see where he worked, an area that was only open to employees, like my father, with government security clearance. That's why I'm here, and I've invited Ric to come with me. I could have not mentioned I was going and instead just wandered through the exhibits and my memories alone, quietly taking notes. But I know Ric has a much better memory of the past than I do, and I need his commentary. Ric and I haven't spent this much time together over the decades since we were kids and he was called "Ricky."

As I follow the cement walkway to the famous Center, bland marigolds bloom in evenly spaced rows, and the mild air and warm sun conspire to make it feel like a real Florida tourist attraction. The swells of welcoming recorded "space" music unfold, as if I were actually moving into and through the black and starry great beyond rather than up to the ticket booth. I can detect the influences of *2001: A Space Odyssey* in the music, and I close my eyes and raise my face toward the sun, floating off in the swelling strings of the mood music with no discernible thematic resolution. By the time Ric returns, I am more than a little edgy and ready to get in line at the ticket kiosk.

"Oh shit," Ric says, patting the front pockets of his jeans as we get to the entrance door. "I forgot about the Mace. I have to go back to the car."

"No way!" I say. "Just discreetly toss it into that garbage can."

"It costs eight bucks."

"So?"

"I'll stash it in the bushes over there," he points to a cement flower planter attached to the side of the building.

"*What?*"

I look around, hoping no one notices what he is doing. What a hassle it would be to get busted hiding a can of Mace in the bushes in front of a federal building, especially with a two-time felon. I can see how he's made some less-than-smart choices over the years, and I can't believe he's not extra careful to avoid doing even the tiniest thing that could land him back in jail.

As we push our tickets into the machines and walk through the Security Clearance turnstiles, the guard says, "One at a time." I imagine this is something my brother has heard before in other situations involving guards.

We pass through the darkened Information Center and wander out into the blazing sunlight of the Rocket Garden. The space music follows. Here, a dozen or so famous missiles, or replicas of missiles, stand at attention on cement pads or lie on their sides, each with a little plaque detailing its merits. *Mercury, Atlas, Titian, Gemini, Apollo, Saturn, Agena*—the names were designed to evoke the grandeur of gods and timelessness.

These missiles are all "old-timers" from the early days of the space industry, the ones launched at the "Old Cape" we will be visiting; at the Space Center, anything before the beginning of the Space Shuttle program in 1981 is considered ancient history. Some of these rockets have been drawn and quartered to reveal their insides and their "stages." Stages, as any Space Coast schoolchild would know, fall off one by one after liftoff, when the missile reaches specific altitudes, until only the main capsule is left.

I wander over to one of the smaller rockets and read it's the Redstone. Redstone is a name I haven't heard in 35 years. The little plaque tells me the sturdy Redstone, the workhorse of the 1950s, was drafted into Project Mercury, NASA's first manned space program in 1958, the year we moved to the area so my father could work at the Cape. *Project Mercury*—how these names come back to me. Alan Shepard rode the *Mercury 7* as the first American in space, my brother reminds me.

"Oh, right," I say.

"And remember that jump-rope thing you and your friends did?" he asks.

"What 'jump-rope thing'?"

"You know, with the names of the seven astronauts."

I don't remember that because I am trying to remember which ones of these missile "corpses" my father might have been a part of. Or rather I am trying to *imagine* which because I don't think I ever knew—and now there is no one left to ask. I think he was part of the Mercury project, so I look for those with that identification. How could a kid not know what rocket her daddy worked on? Isn't that the kind of thing you'd talk about at the dinner table? Wouldn't you actually get kind of sick of hearing about it every night—assuming he was home every night?

I suddenly remember my father worked in guidance, that he was a guidance engineer. Of course, how could I forget? What an ironic job title for him.

I thought I came to visit this tourist site to learn more about the space industry for my writing project. Now I realize I'm searching for my father. I am looking for signs of him I haven't been able to find elsewhere. He has been dead for almost 30 years. I know nothing about his work life, nothing about what he spent his professional career doing—while it lasted—and what he did all day after he drove into the morning traffic jam on that narrow strip of asphalt out to the Cape. I asked him once what he did at work. "Draw pictures," he said in his characteristic, joking tone. I figured out later it had some connection to drafting; in this case, it was drafting a missile flight plan. He was always the go-to guy at home for math and science projects, and he once explained to me "the rule of thumb" about electrical current, but I can't remember it now.

As an inheritance, my dad left me a cardboard, 24-can Schlitz beer box, a nice sturdy one with top flaps that tuck in. He presented it to me rather ceremoniously after alluding to it for years. Like most drunks, he was famous for repeating himself—"That's what you're getting," he would say—but he was also savvy enough to realize the tragedy and irony the legacy of a cardboard box represented. As the oldest and the daughter, I would be the keeper of the family heirlooms.

Inside the box were two slide rules in leather cases from his student years, his Navy medals and a black leather journal from his days as a flight navigator on an aircraft carrier plane during the war, a diploma in electrical engineering from the University of Miami, and a report card from Thomas Junior High in South Philadelphia. There was a collection of postcards, two letters, and greeting cards I sent after I left home, maybe 15 years' worth; it seems I didn't write much. For a guy who made his career tracking missile courses, his course was conspicuously untrackable. Him running out for a pack of Chesterfields when I was a kid could mean two or three days with no sign of his whereabouts.

A couple of tourist kids are dashing down the gangplank to the mock Apollo capsule where they can try out the seats. It was this same kind of gangplank the crew of the Apollo 1 walked down for the launch dress rehearsal, which ended in an accidental flash fire in 1967, killing the three men. My father wasn't there, that I know. By then, he was out of the industry, never to work at the Cape again. One too many drunk-driving arrests and petty misdemeanors meant he lost his all-important, government-issued security clearance. Without it he could no longer drive past the checkpoint gate to get into the Cape. When did that happen, I try to remember. Sometime in the mid-1960s, sometime when I was in high school. I do some quick math and am shocked to realize my father was a rocket engineer for maybe only 10 years.

I appraise the rockets again, this time by launch dates. My brother gives me information, more details than I want to know, about how the missiles work and the peculiarities of some of the components, information he's gleaned from his prodigious reading and watching the Discovery Channel. He takes a professional interest in the welded joints.

The only other visitors in the Rocket Garden besides the kids and their parents are a young couple with shiny new wedding bands, who are taking an inordinate number of photos of each other in front of the rockets. Why are those other people here? I wonder. What can their interest be in these relics? Why would they care that the two things a rocket needs are thrust and guidance? Thrust gets it into the air, and guidance keeps it on its all-important track until it slots into its orbit above the atmosphere.

The Kennedy Space Center is the official name of this tourist attraction, museum, and historical theme park, and it sits just outside the NASA Kennedy Space Center, where the real work of space exploration actually happens. In the early days, all the action was out on the edge of the Cape, until the giant Vehicle Assembly Building and the Space Shuttle launch pads were built farther inland. The Cape Canaveral bus tour is taking us out to see this "old Cape."

At the bus staging area, no fewer than four guards direct us to the right line. There is a wall-sized map mural of where we will be going. Maps are about imagination as much as fact for me, and I imagine the empty green spaces between launch sites still so like the open palmettos I used to wander as a child. We'll be driving over the Banana River and entering through the North Gate; my father always entered through the South Gate, since my hometown of Satellite Beach is south of the Cape.

Once, for a family outing, my father drove us to the South Gate. Since family members without badges weren't allowed, we stopped and gazed for a few moments at the other side where the acres of palmettos looked just like the side we were on. Then he ceremoniously turned the car around. We headed back to Cocoa Beach so we could drive our car along the hard-packed sand with the waves on one side and beachfront joints on the other. We parked and unloaded lawn chairs, beach toys, towels, grill, charcoal, marinated chicken parts, chips, beer, and sodas. We kids headed for the water with my father, who dove headfirst into the waves, a feat I wasn't yet brave enough to try.

Much later, as the evening sky was turning pink and orange, Ric and I scouted for driftwood. My father made a shallow pit behind the car to dump the fading hot coals into while my mother put the food away. My parents drew their chairs around the fire, and Ric and I sat in the sand. Pieces of the wood were added into the pit to flame and flare in the soft darkness, while my father sang all the verses to "A Fox Went Out on a Chilly Night." I sifted the cool night sand through my fingers over and over again, the back of my hand hot from the fire.

With us on the tour bus is a slew of 30-something Russians. What is their interest in this tour, I wonder. Too young to have experienced the Space Race between the Soviet Union and the U.S., they look too hip to not recognize a certain postmodern irony in the situation. After all, the thing we most feared when I was growing up was the Russians invading Cape Canaveral. Maybe these young people read about the Space Race in their textbooks and how the U.S. was actually losing until sometime in the late sixties. That's why there was so much pressure on the Mercury program—to catch up with the Russians and that little dog they sent into orbit.

The bridge arches over the Banana River, and we can look out over the flat expanse of palmetto scrublands surrounding a handful of bare patches with missile sites in the middle of them. We can see the Atlantic stretching all the way to Africa. The guardhouse at the gate waves the bus through since we are all completely security-safe. I wonder if the other tourists are surprised at how much of a wilderness this area really is, less developed than the complex of solid cement of Disney World.

Our tour guide, Dave, tells us that what is now called Cape Canaveral Air Force Station, or the "old Cape," is a mostly natural 17,000 acres, home to alligators and four species of poisonous snakes. Right on cue, we spot a couple of armadillos poking along the side of the road. To me, it's all just beautiful. The sky is as big as I remembered it—like being out on the ocean or in the middle of the Great Plains—and because the weather is on the cool side today, it is bold blue. The gray-green palmettos stretch out as far as can be seen, their rough fronds creating texture against the sky. I suddenly remember the jump-rope rhyme: "Car-penter, Coo-per, Glenn, and Grissom. Schir-ra, Shepard, and Mis-ter Slayton."

Dave fills us in on many facts that involve numbers: dates, speed, thrust, weight, length, numbers of employees, miles around the earth, dollars. Actually, I don't think he ever talks about money, the trillions of dollars spent over the past 50 years maintaining our space superiority. I have figured out that the "now" of this "then and now" tour is about drumming up patriotism, taxpayer interest, and support for the projects now in process for the future.

It's widely recognized that this is the end of a particular kind of era for the Space Center, an era that saw space exploration as a major national interest and funding priority. After this final launch of the Shuttle Atlantis, the expectation is that everything will be privatized. The local *Florida Today* newspaper featured an article on the up-and-coming private companies that will launch missiles for their own interests. The article also reminded us the Space Coast has always seen both boom and bust eras, and it's hard for me to differentiate between the industry's fluctuations in fortune and those of my family.

Dave tells us about the shenanigans of the astronauts when they were in town: the wild parties at the Holiday Inn, the bikinis on Canaveral Pier, the pioneering topless bars, the free Corvettes provided to the astronauts by the enterprising Chevy dealer Jim Rathman, the drag racing down North Atlantic Avenue. But he misses the story about my drunk father somehow driving the 15 miles between Cocoa Beach and our house, skipping the driveway but making a course correction up onto the lawn so that the front bumper of the Chevy just kissed the palm tree before he passed out in the front seat. Dave doesn't say how my mother got me up extra early the next morning to go out to the car to try to get him inside before the neighbors woke up. Or how on occasions when my father didn't make it to the lawn, my mother bundled us kids off to a neighbor's in the middle of the night so she could drive the 20 miles to the mainland to bail him out.

Dave mentions Bernard's Surf as the watering hole where the astronauts and press corps mingled; he doesn't know it's also the bar where my father cashed his paycheck—the paycheck that briefly made us like all the families of Cape engineers, among the highest earners in the state. Dad always left the pile of bills on the bar in front of him so he could tell the bartender to "take it out of there and something for yourself." Whatever was left at the end of the night went into his pocket. My mother and he eventually agreed that the check would be mailed from the payroll office right to our house.

Dave paraphrases the "Vegas rule" to say that back then everyone knew that what happened on the Space Coast stayed on the Space Coast. I wonder, though, what happened if you actually *lived* here? Does what happened just stay there forever?

Our tour passes Hangar "S." Hangar "S" is where the Mercury astronauts prepped for launch, Dave says. Although it's fun to see a famous building we watched on television, I don't really care that much about astronauts; I think my father met a couple of astronauts, officially, at work, but I'm not sure.

What I am most excited to learn, though, is that we are going into the Launch Complex 26 Blockhouse. I have always wanted to go inside a blockhouse, especially one my father might have worked in. They have turned this one, and the surrounding area, into part of the Air Force Space &

Missile Museum, a part that can only be accessed by the special, security-cleared tour we are now on. Nearby is the Launch Complex 5/6 from which Alan Shepard, and later Gus Grissom, were launched on Redstone rockets.

I'm sure this has something to do with my father. I know he spent time in launch blockhouses, and I know, or am pretty sure, he worked on Redstones, at least on the unmanned suborbital missions. Or test firings. Yes, I think he was a test engineer—or maybe that was before he was at the Cape, when he worked for Sperry Gyroscopes in Virginia. It's all so confusing, the numbers and names and places and dates and jargon attached to someone's life, especially someone in the space industry. But I think my father was actually here in this blockhouse—or one very like it.

The tour bus stops in front of the blockhouse and we are told we can wander at will or follow a docent-led tour. I leap up to get off but am still beat by a line in the aisle. Ric is calmly waiting for everyone else to go ahead. He has learned some kind of Zen acceptance somewhere along the way that I missed out on.

The Russians are chattering among themselves as they stoop to peer out the bus windows at the white, squat cement building with the slight igloo hump for a roof. We have already learned that the walls are 2 feet thick while the roof varies between 5 and 8 feet. The sun hits me in the face as I make the final step off the bus; I had forgotten how forceful and ubiquitous the sunshine is here.

The docent swings open one side of the double blast-doors, a heavily plated gateway to a 20th-century fortress. Like the entrance to a cave, the narrow entryway opens into a small chamber, large enough for a dozen or so people to stand comfortably and is decorated with rocket "cheesecake" photos. On either side, doors lead into the two firing rooms, the control rooms from where the rockets were launched, where the buttons were *actually pushed* to fire up the engines.

We learn that everything in the firing rooms—control panels, equipment, lighting fixtures, wiring paths, paint schemes—is original. The buttons and control handles are cute, looking almost like toys with their rounded, braised-metal edges, shaped and sized for mere 20th-century humans just cutting their first space baby teeth. The black buttons stamped with numbers look like the keys on an old-fashion typewriter. On the front of the control panels are tiny pullout ashtrays like the one in my father's 1954 Chevy. Inside are cigarette butts, original cigarette butts, the docent tells us. Like a child, I imagine that maybe one is my father's—but then I see it is a Lucky Strike, not a Chesterfield.

Two blue-green slits, like reptile eyes, look out at the launch pads only 400 feet away. The window glass is comprised of 42 layers of quarter-inch glass. Forty-two layers of mica-thin glass, laid one on top of the other very carefully, then heat-fused into a solid block. Even though I can see through it, the view is fuzzy and only the big, outlined shape of a rocket, or a palm tree—or a man's life with the hot fiery blastoff of anger obscuring everything else—can be seen before the shape slowly rises.

I see the Burroughs guidance computer, identical to the two installed in the Radio Guidance Center. I associate the words "radio" and "guidance" and "test" with my father; he was a radioman on a Navy plane, after all, and a test engineer at another point. I've heard the word "Burroughs" sometime in the past, the way children hear those grown-up words without knowing their meaning and then repeat them knowingly. I read these computers were used to control the rocket's flight, using five receiving dishes and transmitting guidance commands back to the rocket. In later years, my father mentioned he used some of the first computers back in the day, the big clunky kind. Indeed, the docent tells us, "The processing computers on board a Mercury mission are now available in a thirty-dollar wristwatch." I stare at the long brown metal machine, vaguely rusting, but receive no messages from it.

I wander outside into the sleepy Florida afternoon. Some tourists are still inside asking questions, and others are sitting on the benches overlooking the Rocket Garden; the tour guide and bus driver are jawing with a couple of the docents. I walk out into the St. Augustine grass, carefully watching for sticker burrs, and sit down on a chunk of cement. Some kind of bird calls from the palmettos in the late-afternoon light.

I try to make up a story, a story not about what was, but a story composed of "what ifs" and "as ifs," a story that makes my father something other than a minor engineer on a big project who drank his way out of a security clearance. In this story he is not the father who didn't come home at night. Instead, he is the kind of father who brought us out here on one of those Saturdays in the 1960s when they briefly opened the Cape so the families could see Daddy's rockets. In this story he is a father like one of those on television who dispensed loving guidance to his kids after work.

Too sappy, I think. It can just be an ordinary story. My father would be a regular guy who does his job well, maybe gets singled out from time to time for his good work. He can still be the hail-good-fellow kind of guy who others greet in the hall, who always has a joke or a story to tell. Buck, a great guy, a four-square guy, who maybe in later years the younger men call "Mr. Buckmaster" until he tells them to just call him Buck. And at home, he will really play the mandolin, not just a few chords, stopping with a "hee-hee" when he messes up.

"What are you doing?" My brother is suddenly beside me.

"Nothing." I realize this is an answer I have given before to my family when interrupted while in the middle of one of my stories. "So what's up with all the knives?" I ask him.

"My knives? It's just my pocket knife. And the Leatherman has a little knife on it."

A Leatherman, a pocket multipurpose tool in case he needs to fix something along the way, like our father would have carried.

We rejoin the tour group. Dave winds up again. A jackrabbit dashes across the crumbling, nearly abandoned, road. We are headed toward the launch pad, site of the disastrous Apollo 1 fire.

"The next stop, folks," Dave says, "is hallowed ground."

Bingo Territory

Marion Starling Boyer

River Teeth, 2016

My husband and I have seen too much grimness lately, managing our parents' care. Long corridors, steam trays, wheelchairs. To escape Michigan's bitter winter and the bite of age, we drive to Florida for the month of February. We're trying out a retirement mobile-home community. Discreet signs indicate that it's "Deed Restricted," meaning if you're younger than fifty-five or have kids, live elsewhere.

We're renting a double-wide "manufactured home." The word "trailer" draws frowns. Neat sidewalks line streets named for flowers. We live on Delphinium. Everyone who walks or bicycles by waves. The women have that bobbed-hair-capri-pants-and-T-shirt kind of breeziness. To me, it looks vaguely reminiscent of a 1950s postcard of the Community of the Future, just before the nuclear cloud burst.

There's a heated pool and clubhouse. We can join the morning water aerobics class or sign up for bocce ball and bingo. There's beginning harmonica and a manifestation class, in which we are invited to "manifest peace, harmony, and prosperity." Next Sunday is a party for anyone in the park from Michigan. We're encouraged to "wear Michigan clothes," but I'm not sure if that means University of Michigan, something touting any Michigan location, or a parka, scarf, boots, and mittens. I sign up to bring dessert. We declined the pancake breakfast, and a few heads tilted, brows furrowed. Maybe going to the Michigan party will make up for that.

A brief car ride takes us to Venice Beach, where the major diversion is to hunt for fossilized shark teeth. The beach is known for this oddity—shark teeth continually wash up here by the thousands. They are jet black, usually in a Y shape, and small enough to fit on a nickel. Everyone ambles the beach, head down, often pausing to examine a tiny bit, then pocket it or cast it aside. My husband and I find eleven shark teeth in one hour's walk. We're disproportionately proud of ourselves. It feels like a very productive afternoon. We're keeping the teeth in a jar so we have something to show for ourselves.

We visit "The Dome," a nearby produce and flea-market park. A man sells fish from a chipped red cooler, and there are some bins with fruit and vegetables. Beyond that are stalls with jewelry made from crystals, assorted wallets and handbags, secondhand furniture, tables of athletic socks, used paperbacks, and plastic visors. Roundish couples browse. We are one more wandering couple in the mob. I feel claustrophobic and escape to the jammed parking lot.

In the afternoon we enter Bealls Department Store, and color explodes against my eyes. All the colors from Michigan's clothes washed out and drained down to Florida. Coral, turquoise, peach, lime, rose, melon. Dazzled, I pile up four pair of the same capri pants, thinking of course I'll wear the same pants in yellow, green, aqua, and pink! Oh! Look! Coordinating shirts! And wow! Matching hats! Handbags! Thirty percent off. And! This is "senior day" with an additional discount! My husband wants to know how long I'll be. Should he stay or wait in the car?

Why are we doing everything together? We hunt shark teeth together. We grocery shop together. We negotiate unfamiliar routes together. We peck away at our laptops. Together. We never do this at home and have come to realize each other's habits are unfathomably time-consuming and pointless.

I turn sixty-five this month and will celebrate far away from our children. My husband and I will search out a lovely restaurant near water and choose some kind of fish. We will order wine or an umbrella drink. The restaurant will be crowded. We will eat without anything to say to one another.

I want this Florida trial to be good. I want to think, ah, we can do this again every winter when we are glum from the overcast sky and fed up with snow. I want to imagine I will enjoy my older years in a safe, clean environment, a tidy home that is a delight to decorate with sea-glass and white-washed furniture. Residents ask when we're going to buy a mobile.

They grin and tell us how they rented at first and then, boy, that was it, this is the life!

"We had to gut our place when we bought, but it's fun making it over. Yesterday I found a dresser for sixteen dollars. It'll be perfect when I paint it white," a woman chirps at the Michigan party.

The women swap stories about roaming garage sales and home-goods stores for cunning items that fit their nautical or tropical color schemes. A friend and I drop in on an acquaintance's mobile that looks like it's been torn from Pottery Barn's catalog. Nothing is out of place. The rooms are decorated in aquas and blues with glossy dark wood floors and bright white walls.

After we leave my friend tells me, "She makes her half of the bed right when she gets up, even if her husband is still sleeping."

"Her place is beautiful, but you don't want to live in a magazine, do you?" I say.

"Yes," she sighs, "I do."

It is pretty here, like a stage backdrop, or a postcard with "Wish you were here!" emphatically scripted across a sunset. I feel anxious and disoriented.

Then I meet a woman who doesn't spend hours at Home Goods or Tuesday Morning. Her mobile is not thematic. She's painted crazy rings of color up the palm tree growing in her yard. An end table holds a mannequin's torso decoupaged with magazine pages. On her walls are several five-foot-long fish she's made from dead palm fronds. They're painted in a riot of spots and squiggles, stripes and circles, and every fish has eyelashes. I clap my hands and hurry from room to room deciding if the coral, yellow, and green fish is my favorite or the blue one with lifesaver rings and a lime back.

Now this has become my mission: I drive everywhere examining undergrowth to see which palm variety sheds fronds suitable to become fish. It is satisfying to have purpose. I ignore the facts that I hate to paint anything and they will be impossible to get home. I load up the car several times. I heap the huge stiff fronds in the driveway for my husband to admire.

He's tentative. He's glad I'm happy. He refrains from saying more, as it might tip a balance, because now I have hives. Not sunburn, not blistering, but itchy bumps along my jaw, shoulders, my neck, and across my lower back, which has not seen the light of day since years began with the number nineteen.

This is my first birthday when I am alive and my mother is not. She died at ninety-one. Her mother died at the same age. So, the odds are I have twenty-six more winters ahead, and I think it is too many.

My husband suggests we drive to Casey Key. Here, an hour before sunset, thirty or more drummers gather to beat out rhythms complicated and tribal. We unpack our chairs, a small picnic, and walk to the beach. There are more than a thousand people here, seated in folding chairs with bottles of wine and sophisticated appetizers. This is not a chips-and-dip crowd. I see sushi, imported cheeses, strawberries dipped in chocolate.

Women belly dance in the center of the circled onlookers. Bangles flash and glint. Girls twirl hula hoops. A woman floats in wearing a gossamer cape she swings and billows, her face beatific.

It is circus and ceremony. Children sashay in the sand. The drummers half-close their eyes, maybe chant. Drums drum on. Five women join hands and writhe together in a way that looks ancient and sisterly.

A thin, deeply tanned man crouches, solemnly holds a large dream catcher out toward the sea, then swishes it in a large circle above his head. He appears intent and serious, committed and completely silly. Another man slides through slow poses of t'ai chi, glancing out the corners of his eyes to see if he's noticed. A sailboat anchors picturesquely off shore, perfect as an advertisement.

Clouds stretch and blush. The molten sun lowers. Like an Aztec ritual, onlookers rise, move to the water's edge, raise high their phones and iPads. Everyone watches the horizon as though it's never happened before, as though it will never happen again.

The Life and Death (and Life) of Miami Beach

Jennifer S. Brown

An old racetrack once stood majestically at the tip of Miami Beach, a buffer zone between the ocean out there and the land in here. It was a place, according to a 1939 WPA guidebook, that attracted "the playboy and plowboy, the dowager in pearls and the sylph in shorts, the banker on vacation and the grifter on prowl." Miami Beach in its heyday, a young seductress, tempting the world. And this track symbolized it all.

Of course, knowing that it was actually a dog track, the Biscayne Track, takes away a little of its glamour. It perched right across the street from Joe's Stone Crab. Joe's Stone Crab is another Miami Beach landmark, the city's first restaurant, in existence since 1913. I've wondered how Joe's has thrived for so long on Miami Beach, which has always been heavily populated by Jews. Stone crabs are about as kosher as ham and cheese with mayo on white bread.

I suppose, though, that if it didn't bother my own Jewish grandparents, then it must not have bothered anyone else's either. Somehow in Miami Beach, the rules have always been pliable.

I loved going to Joe's Stone Crab—according to my father, who I admit has been wrong on occasion, Joe's owns all the crabbing boats so its stone crabs are the best, succulent and juicy. My family only went to Joe's when my grandparents would take us. Joe's has never taken reservations, and the wait for a table could last up to three hours. All the waiters were older men who walked stiffly, carrying trays laden with the chilled orange legs of stone crabs. When we went, we followed a precise routine, as unvaried as "Who's on First." My grandfather would go up to the maître d' and slip him an undisclosed amount of money. I'd peer but my grandfather was too slick, and I could never see the money actually changing hands. My cousin and I would debate how big the bribe was. Twenty dollars? Fifty? My grandfather would return to us, giving my father a little nod and a grin. Then my grandmother would say—every time—"We're never going to get a table. It's going to take forever," to which my grandfather would say, "Don't worry. It won't be long." And sure enough, moments later, "Kapelow, party of six" (and it never mattered how large a party we were— sometimes with friends and other family members we were as many as 16) would boom over the microphone and we'd bypass envious tourists still propped against walls, sliding onto the floor, or leaning on any piece of furniture close to them.

I never went to the dog track. Like many Miami Beach relics, it closed years before I was old enough to enter.

What can be said about a city like Miami Beach? A city whose spoil is- lands—those islands in Biscayne Bay created by the leftover dredgings from the making of Miami Beach—were wrapped in pink plastic by the artist Christo. A city that once had someone run for mayor on the platform that he'd build a replica of Jerusalem's Western Wall on Lincoln Road Mall. A city that has a string skirting its perimeter, an eruv, so the Orthodox Jews can consider all of South Beach their neighborhood, allowing them to carry things on Shabbat. A city in which I have yet to figure out when the bars are required to close because I have yet to see one with its doors shut.

Watching most cities age is like watching your parents age. On a day-to-day basis, nothing seems to change. Your parents look the same, sound the same. But go away—to summer camp, to college, to a distant city—and upon return, you're shocked at the differences. Have your father's shoul- ders always stooped? Is that a new set of wrinkles around your mother's mouth? When did their hair turn so gray?

Watching Miami Beach age, though, is more like having a wealthy grand- mother. When you return, her hair is a brighter shade of gold. Her skin is tauter and smooth. Her teeth are white and strong.

And Miami Beach is certainly a vain old woman. Forty-five years ago, her face, pockmarked with wrinkles and sags, revealed her age to her em- barrassment, even though, unlike other grand cities, she was less than 70 years old. She had spent too many years in the sun and her skin had turned a leathery brown, with signs of melanoma. But Miami Beach is a *rich* old woman, and she has been able to afford a facelift. While other women have augmented their chests, Miami Beach has scooped from the bottom of the ocean, digging up sand to augment her beaches, even though, like many old women, Miami Beach was advised this would be hazardous to her health. But what's the worry about vulnerability in hurricanes and the negative environmental impact, when your appearance is at stake? While other women have had the skin tightened on their faces to obliterate the wrinkles, Miami Beach has sand-blasted the surfaces of her old buildings to obliterate the eyesores. While other woman have pumped collagen into their faces to round out the rough edges, Miami Beach has pumped in money, gentrifying neighborhoods, turning out the natives.

But then, what is a native in a city that is completely man-made?

In the beginning, Miami Beach was wilderness. Tremendous growths of vegetation stood on a sandbar in the Atlantic. Carl Fisher is the man credited with making Miami Beach an entity. In 1912, Fisher visited the land that had previously failed to serve as coconut plantations, and apparently saw potential in, as the WPA guidebook described, the "1,600-acre, jungle-matted sand bar." His wife, Jane, thought differently. As she wrote of Miami Beach, "an old alligator roared its resentment . . . the mosquitoes were biting every exposed inch of me . . . the jungle itself was as hot and steamy as a conservatory . . . I refused to find any charm in this deserted strip of ugly land . . . It was Carl's greatest and craziest dream."

My father vacationed in Miami Beach when he was just 5, in the summer of 1945. His mother and he came to stay with my namesake, his Aunt Jennie, who lived at the Avalon Hotel. The lobby was the only part of the hotel that was air-conditioned, and his room was brutally hot. In the mornings, he'd drink fresh orange juice from Leo's and every night he'd have dinner at Emil's. In the mornings, he and the other kids, Kathleen, Neil, Morty, and Sheldon (my father is one of those strange sorts who remembers every detail of every event in his life) would play a game where they'd guess where everyone went to dinner. They'd always start with my father, saying, "You went to Emil's," then continue trying to guess where everyone else went. This was a tremendous disappointment to my father. On rare occasions, he'd get to go to Pickin' Chicken, which my father still claims is the best fried chicken he's ever tasted. Breakfast and lunch were eaten at one of the cafeterias, Cadillac's or Hoffman's. None of these exist anymore. During the days, my dad played with the other kids on the beach, occasionally going into the water. He didn't like to go in too often because his mother, afraid he'd get earaches, made him wear a shower cap.

"You know," my father told me on the phone, "we had a semi-famous person staying at the hotel that summer. Do you remember who Dinah Shore was? Well, her cousin, Clarence, was living at the Avalon."

People *lived* at the Avalon. In the off-season of July, their cheapest room is $227. Not terribly expensive, but a bit out of reach if you wanted to make the hotel your home.

Miami Beach was not born but created. Created as a glamorous, sultry playground for the rich. The wealthy swarmed to the South to play in the speakeasies, Miami Beach seemingly unaffected by Prohibition. Strictly exclusive, signs were posted on the northern part of the beach: "No Jews or dogs." Strange, then, that after the Great Depression and the advent of World War II, Miami Beach became, in effect, a shtetl, a place for middle-class Jews who were barred from the ritzier New York resorts. And during this time, South Beach grew, adopting the style that would define this part of town: Art Deco. Art Deco is a funky form, with bold strokes, zigzaggy lines, and geometric shapes. Add to this pastel colors and you have the Beach. Anyone who can't picture this need only to watch an old episode of *Miami Vice*.

Miami Beach faltered, though. Like any fad, Miami Beach became a place for the untrendy, the unhip. It became a place for retirees. Many of the Art Deco buildings were torn down to make high-rises, but the area to the south was neglected, once-majestic buildings were allowed to crumble. In the 1980s, this area became a slum, a place where the Marielitos made their homes, frightening the then-elderly Jews who lived on South Beach, causing many to leave. The Marielitos were the Cubans who came over in 1980. When President Carter welcomed the Cubans who snuck into the States, Castro retaliated by opening up the port of Mariel and letting anyone who wanted flee to the United States. He also opened up his prisons and mental institutions, ridding his country of some of its worst criminals. As a result, Miami was flooded with 125,000 Cubans, overwhelming the unprepared city. According to T. D. Allman, in his book *Miami: City of the Future,* the vast majority were "law-abiding citizens." However, about 10,000 of them were extremely violent and after the boat lifts, the crime rate in South Florida rose tremendously. In a *New York Times* article, Judge Thomas A. Testa called life in this southern part of Miami Beach "subhuman." It was "a breeding place for crime and a place where residents [were] afraid to walk at night and prostitutes from the mainland gravitate[d] because of the cheap hotels."

My mother's first trip to Miami Beach was in 1953, when she was 8. Unlike my father's family, her family was well-to-do, and they stayed at the Fontainebleau Hotel, then the classiest place on the Beach. She spent time at the Kitty Pool, a cat-shaped children's wading pool that had whiskers and a tail painted on the tiles. Her father took off for a few nights to Cuba, where he spent his time smoking expensive cigars and gambling.

The Kitty Pool was eliminated when they remodeled at the hotel. And hopping from Miami Beach to Cuba isn't so common. And it's now the Fontainebleau Hilton.

Barbara Capitman is credited with almost single-handedly saving the Art Deco district. In the late 1970s and early 1980s she petitioned to make the area a historical landmark. Many fought her, mostly developers who wanted to raze the area and build more high-rises. One of her most outspoken opponents was Abe Resnick, a developer and city commissioner, who said, "I love old buildings. But these Art Deco buildings are 40, 50 years old. They aren't historic. They aren't special. We shouldn't be forced to keep them." Capitman won. The Art Deco district was born.

Now, Miami Beach is trendy once again, a place for celebrities and foreigners, a place where gays are not only welcomed but courted. New restaurants, clubs, and shops are popping up every day. When the first Starbucks went in about 20 years ago, my father excitedly gave me updates on the progress, which went up too slowly for his caffeinated tastes. As New York magazine put it, Miami Beach was "the SoHo of the South."

People were paying millions for dilapidated hotels, renovating them for the Europeans and weekending New Yorkers. The Art Deco district flourished in its revival. Aren't those investors sorry they didn't get in on the ground floor? In 1915, Carl Fisher was offering beach property for free— absolutely nothing—to anyone who was willing, or rather crazy enough, to settle it.

My senior prom was held in the Eden Roc hotel. At one time, the Eden Roc was high-class. After all, if you remember, Lucy and Ricky Ricardo stayed there in the episodes where they vacationed in Miami Beach. The Eden Roc was glamour—women in gloves and men who wore hats. In 1986, it was crawling with high-schoolers, more anxious to get to an upstairs room than to play out any roles of sophistication. The Eden Roc went desperately out of style, as did the Fontainebleau next door, becoming a place for families and the elderly on their visits from Long Island. The glamour and allure now beckoned from Ocean Drive. Though with a few investors, a spanking-new spa, and a revitalization, no one is holding senior proms there anymore.

"Necco wafer–colored" and "cotton candy–colored" are just a few of the terms used to describe Miami Beach. I can't exactly disagree. The Miami Beach I know now leaves a syrupy-sweet taste in mouth, so perhaps the descriptions are even more apt than I originally thought.

Did you know that Miami Beach has the only Art Deco Burger King in the country? It's light pink and pastel green.

Miami Beach and Miami are separate, distinct cities. Miami Beach is charmed—it hasn't felt many of the pressures facing Miami. The riots didn't touch Miami Beach. Hurricane Andrew mangled only a few trees on the Beach. The character of the Beach is different from Miami. Miami is business and formality. Miami Beach is ocean and fun. When someone questions a family member on where we're from, and he or she simply replies, "Miami," I become defensive, adding, "Miami *Beach*." It's easier to just say Miami; it needs less explaining. I'd rather explain.

Maybe I'm defensive because I actually lived between the two, on the Venetian Causeway, a small two-lane toll road connecting Miami and Miami Beach. It's a quiet road—the toll has steadily been rising and is now $2.25 to cross—dwarfed by the MacArthur Causeway to the south and Julia Tuttle Causeway to the north. Six islands—although when I say islands I imagine people are envisioning white beaches, palm trees, a gentle surf; the island my family lives on is a slab of concrete plopped down in Biscayne Bay—grace the causeway; you can even see them if you look at a state map. The island I lived on is not the patrolled, gated community of Palm Island or Hibiscus Island or even Star Island. The island I lived on is small and the population was divided into two classes: the well-off and the better-off; those who lived across the street from the water on the inner strip of landlocked pavement and those who lived on the water. My family lived on the inside. The difference between a house on the inside and a house on the water is about $2 million. The difference is the blue, stick-shift Rabbit I was occasionally allowed to drive to school *if* I had a special reason, and the brand-new Mercedes my friend across the street got for his 15th birthday. The difference is JCPenney at the mall and Neiman Marcus at Bal Harbour.

Like proud parents who can't see how ugly their child really is, I defend Miami Beach no matter how ridiculous I sound. "Oh, sure," I've been known to say, "the crime rate was high when I was living there. But I was a kid! It didn't touch me." The funny thing is, I believe it, until I think of little things. Like that my father's car was broken into three times—each time in our own driveway. Like the night in ninth grade when my mother came downstairs to wake me up at close to 3:00 a.m. on a school night.

"Jen, hon, wake up."

"Huh?" I mumbled exhausted, as I had only gone to sleep an hour before, having spent the entire night talking on the phone with Natalie, trying to decide if the look Richard had given me that day in between fourth and fifth periods had meant anything significant.

"Come upstairs, now," she said quietly.

My first thought was, the house is on fire. But then it occurred to me, you don't go upstairs when there's a fire; you leave the house.

"What is it?" I asked, but my mother put her finger over her lips as we walked up, gesturing toward my sister's room, which was next to hers.

She brought me into her bedroom; my father was still lying in bed, unconcerned. "I was worried," my mother said. "I was afraid you might hear a noise, turn on a light, and become a target." She pulled me to the far side of the room and pointed out the window. The house across the street was visible under the streetlight. Swarming around the house were a number of cars and about 15 men carrying rifles. My mother didn't let me look for long.

To my disappointment, nothing happened. I fell asleep upstairs.

But the next day, the *Miami Herald* reported that those men were cops, DEA agents. The guy who lived across the street had been laundering money for some drug kingpins. Apparently, the cops thought he'd be coming home that night but he never showed. They ended up picking him up at the airport.

My parents had been worried about the event. I only felt cheated that I didn't get to see anything actually go down.

I used to hear, "You grew up in Miami Beach? I didn't think people actually lived there." Then what I got was, "I didn't realize you were Cuban." Now, people say, "Wow, how cool!" I went to a school we called Beach High, only that didn't sound strange to us. While relatives in the North had snow days, I distinctly remember our riot days. In particular, when they announced the verdict in the trial of a Hispanic officer accused of killing an African American motorcyclist. I spent the day at Ellen Horowitz's with about six friends, watching *The World According to Garp* on cable and eating raw cookie dough. I remember this because Josh Bloom and I were sort of trying to get back together in that way that 10th-graders do, circling around, feeling each other out, neither wanting to be the first to say anything. Come to think of it, that's still the way I do it. Anyway, nothing came from that verdict. In fact, to show what little significance this event played in my life, I'm embarrassed to admit I can't even remember if the officer was innocent or guilty. But that was life on Miami Beach. It wasn't a thrilling city; it was home.

My mother, an artist, loved the changes in Miami Beach for a while. And why shouldn't she? Everyone did. The art community was flourishing, there were more places to socialize, everything became just so, well, colorful.

But doesn't anyone else miss the quiet Miami Beach? The Miami Beach where you could ride your bike down Ocean Drive and be greeted by rows of elderly Jews sitting on the porches of old hotels, just staring at the water. These were the survivors, the tough ones, the ones who still spoke with Yiddish accents and hid the numbers etched on their arms. The city tucked these people away, replacing them with the young, the hip. After all, gay New Yorkers are much more entertaining. The elderly haven't been completely forgotten—an ugly green hand rises from the ground just off Dade Boulevard as a testament, a Holocaust memorial. A monument so tacky and hideous that my mother can't help but refer to it as the Arm of the Jolly Green Giant. We should remember the elderly; we just shouldn't have to look at them.

I confess, when I still lived in Miami Beach, I relished the changes. Life was getting fun. No longer was I confined to Blackie's on the Beach for drinking with friends. I had a world of options. When Club Nu opened during my freshman year of college, I rejoiced. Finally somewhere to go dancing on the Beach.

When I moved to New York, my father and I played a game. He'd ask me, "Is the such and such still on 14th Street?" or "Is such and such deli still on First Avenue?" and I'd tell him, "No, a Bargain Basement moved in there" or whatever had transpired. Occasionally, very occasionally, something would remain, and my father would feel connected to a city he hadn't lived in for more than 20 years.

Now, I walk through Miami Beach and ask, "What's that?" while pointing to a new café. "Where's Butterflake Bakery? What happened to Art Barker's newsstand?" I hold on to what still remains, no longer recognizing my former home.

Miami Beach is a haven for models. The warm weather, beaches, and days besotted with sunshine make it a year-round spot for outdoor shoots. The Europeans love to use it for catalogue work. And of course, ever since Michael Mann brought *Miami Vice* to the city, the film business has skyrocketed. I remember going away for my freshman year at the University of Texas, when every Friday night the Miami Beach contingent (and there were quite a few of us: the school lured many good students with tremendous scholarships; I was there because they had no application form—just a bubble sheet to fill out) would gather around the TV and thrill at Sonny Crockett and Ricardo Tubbs. We'd drink every time we noticed a continuity error—errors only a native could spot. "Hey," I'd shout, excitedly downing my tequila shot, "they're going the wrong way on the Venetian Causeway. They're headed toward the Beach, not the airport." I have to admit, I watched more than once Michael Mann's atrocious movie of teenaged delinquents, *Band of the Hand*, because in the opening sequence, they blew up my high school. In fact, if you watch the movie today, you can get an idea of what South Beach looked like—old, run-down, dangerous, and beautiful.

But now, riding my mother's bike down Ocean Drive, I feel like a tourist. My skin, dark by northern standards, is white among the beach population—something I've gone to great strides to maintain with layers of SPF 45—and there's no way I'd ever wear a bikini. Everyone is beautiful and young—and I mean even younger than me or at least they've had enough plastic surgery to give that illusion. I remember when I'd walk down the street and the old people in the hotels would gush at how beautiful I was. Now, I'm all but invisible to the part-time residents of the glamour hotels.

The city has gone too far. The real estate values have risen at incredible rates. The artists can no longer afford their quaint Lincoln Road studios. The quirky Jewish bakeries and Cuban shops have long been forced out, replaced by Banana Republic and Pottery Barn. In this sense, Miami Beach is becoming like every other city in the country. The mom-and-pop stores are disappearing. Miami Beach is falling like Coconut Grove once did. Coconut Grove used to be a refuge for artists, full of foliage and pretty streets to window-shop. Now, it's one big outdoor mall.

The dog track, apparently, was just another wrinkle on the face of Miami Beach. Now, South Pointe Tower condominiums and South Pointe Park stand where the dog track once presided. Joe's Stone Crab expanded, more than doubling its size, which is a good thing considering that the maître d's got caught by the local news for taking bribes to seat people faster. I think I even saw a female waiter the last time I went. As my father says, "Miami Beach was once a place to be. Now it's a place to be seen."

I still return every year, for two weeks at New Year's. But now I bring my kids with me. And to them, Miami Beach is one great big play yard. The Parrot Jungle of my youth, birds flying everywhere, is now the antiseptic Jungle Island, a stone's throw from my parents' new condo on Belle Isle. Lincoln Road isn't an artistic outing, but where we get ice cream from the Frieze and shop the post-Christmas sales at the Gap. Today my kids are playing on the train at Flamingo Park. Tomorrow they'll be heading to the club du jour. I'm an outsider now. Miami Beach is theirs, the birthright of the young. But still, no matter how much surgery she may have, underneath the gobs of makeup the old lady remains. Miami Beach once home, always home.

Miami Beach is dead. Long live Miami Beach.

Florida Vacation

An Essay in Third Person

Jill Christman

Superstition Review, 2011

She was in the grocery store sulking past forbidden sugar cereals when she stopped, looked around, and realized she could put a box of Froot Loops in her cart if she wanted. Could she? She was 34 years old. She did. Nobody stopped her—who would stop her?—but she kept checking her back until she made it out to the parking lot and got all the bags into the car.

At home, the milk turned a putrid gray, and even dry, the bright sugar rings weren't as good as she remembered them. She sat at the wooden table in the kitchen with the baby, sliding the red ones into place for the top arc of a cereal rainbow and remembering the Atari her brother had won back in the mid-seventies with his drawing of Toucan Sam in the Kellogg's "Stick up for Breakfast" contest. The only game was Pong, a drifting dot and two straight-line paddles locked in a perpetual bling-boing-bling. How would she ever communicate to her new-millennium daughter the excitement, the *thrill*, of the day that Atari arrived in its plain brown box? For months, her brother—celebrated artist, creator of the winning Sam-in-the-jungle scene—reigned as king of the neighborhood.

She was down to the greens in her ROY G. BIV rainbow when she realized something, something big: They could catch a plane. They could buy tickets, fly out of dreary, frozen Indiana and celebrate the rest of Christmas vacation somewhere sunny—and alone. This was revelatory. A full year into her daughter's life and Jill suddenly understood that *she* was the mother.

She chose a family-run hotel in Madeira Beach near St. Petersburg. Their room had a little kitchen with one of those undersized stoves and a too-bright fluorescent light, but the double glass doors looked out over the bay where the proprietor seemed always to be busy on his sailboat, *Island Woman*. That's the thing about men and their boats, she thought—they can never get enough. There's always something to fiddle with, a reason to pull her out of the water, sink her back in, sand her down, shine her up. A man with a boat never lacks for something to do.

Her own husband, boatless, was still sleeping in the king-sized bed under the giant straw fan, and Jill sat cross-legged next to the baby tossing Cheerios onto the tray of her booster chair. They faced the water and the man. Boat TV. A pelican—the baby's first!—sailed in and landed hard on a piling. "Look, Ella! Look! A pelican!" She could have called that bird anything—a sea gull, a loon, or an osprey, an ostrich for heavensakes—and the baby would have believed her. But she didn't. She called it a pelican.

That afternoon, they set up the booster chair on a picnic table and drank margaritas and ate blackened grouper sandwiches on the dock. The baby munched fries and smeared ketchup in her hair. Men in tight suits buzzed by in weird parachute machines that reminded her of the jet-pack police in *Fahrenheit 451*. A gull dove down to steal a fry and her husband covered his head with his hands, threatened to scream like a little girl. That night was New Year's Eve and she fell asleep on the couch in front of the glass doors despite the blasts of color exploding over the water. Her husband woke her up with a midnight kiss just as Regis talked the ball down in Times Square (*Regis? Where's Dick Clark?*) and they went together into the bedroom to kiss their sleeping angel on her fat cheeks. She felt a kind of surreal happiness and thought, *This is probably as good as it gets.*

The next afternoon, while the other two napped, Jill took her book down to the dock to show her Indiana-white legs to the Florida sun, breathe in some air the wind had cleaned on the salty water. She was never alone these days. She found a spot on a bench and another sea plane pelican, all pouch and hold, skimmed low across the water, eyes trained down, look-ing to scoop up some morsels, swallow them whole and squirming. From a distance, the pelican had seemed so exotic. Up close, she could see the pelican was filthy, mangy. A dirty bird.

Her book wasn't even cracked before a little girl came skipping down the planks of the dock on her bare feet and cast a towel in a flap of rainbow colors down on the warm wood.

"Mmm," the girl said. "I think I'll set up *here* for awhile!" She was 6, she reported, her name was Cameron, and she was here in Florida with her mom and dad for a whole *week*. After this they'd go to see her sister's *baby* who had just learned to walk. Cameron wanted to know if Jill had any sisters or babies and she told her, feeling lucky, that she had both. *Two sisters and one baby, my own little girl, also one, who's sleeping up in the room.* Cameron took that in, told her that Ella was a good name, and then mentioned the brother she never sees. He was in some kind of trouble, she wasn't sure. She'd like to see all of them more—the sister with the baby, the baby, the brother—but she was careful to let Jill know they don't all live together. They can't. They live all over the country. *All* over the coun-try. Jill noticed Cameron's flare for emphasis, one word in every sentence, often where she'd least expect it.

As Cameron talked, lying on her belly, her bare feet stirred the air in rapid circles and her palms patted the colors of her towel. Every paragraph or two, she required a bit of information. "Do you have any *brothers*?"

"Yes," Jill reported, "and he has a little girl exactly your age." Jill's eyes flicked up to the mother lying by the kidney-shaped pool, a pool only big enough for children to really get going in, but beautiful in a tropical way, palm trees and shine. The mother looked to be about 40, so she would have been about her age when she had Cameron. Not a young mother. The other mother's sunglasses pointed down toward her book. An older man sat two lounge chairs away, talking business on a cell phone—probably almost 60, and that explained the sister with the baby, the brother too far away to see, maybe in some kind of trouble . . .

Cameron popped up from her towel, all long brown legs and round eyes. She couldn't stay down for long. She was made of springs and tendons. "Well," she said, "I guess I'd better *throw* these shells back in the water so they can become sand!" She produced a handful of shells out of nowhere, scuttled to the edge of the dock, still chattering about the fish she saw earlier, bigger than these little fish, *much* bigger, but *look* at all those fish now. Do you *see* them? And she cast the shells, a handful of tiny white shells, like beads or confetti, across the calm surface of the water and they sprayed down, a lovely sprinkle of sound. Together they watched them sink down through interested fish and onto the sandy bottom. "Watch," Cameron instructed, "now watch." And the sand on the bottom shifted and danced—was it moving all that time? before the shells?—and Cameron's luminescent shells absorbed into the tawny grains. "See? See? Now they will become sand."

Although she'd be loath to confess, Jill wasn't always one to enjoy the company of other people's children, but she liked this Cameron. She sparkled, but the way she talked to her was terrifying. Jill found herself wishing she wouldn't tell her so much. There's too much not to trust in this world, and strange ladies sitting on docks are probably one of them. Also, there was something behind her eyes, something old. Something that reminded her of herself.

Her husband walked down to the dock carrying the baby. Ella squinted into the bright light to marvel at the lively creature standing on the dock next to her mother, so much better than a pelican. "This is *my* baby," she told Cameron. "This is Ella." Cameron reached out for Ella's cheeks and pinched them just as an old woman might do. Ella hated to be pinched, but she didn't cry. Cameron's eyes were too round. Too much like her own eyes.

With a bigger audience, Cameron turned businesslike, played the experienced tourist. After all, they'd been there for a week. She gave her review of the Dali museum. At first, they heard "dolly" because she was six, but their misimpression didn't last long. "You have to touch the fur when you first go in. It's red. You have to touch it." Cameron was full of instructions. "Then you look into this box and it's like a frame. Inside it's a face, but it's not a face. There are two pictures on the wall and they're the eyes. Then there's a fire. That's the nose. And a couch is the mouth."

For the rest of the afternoon, Cameron trailed Jill and the baby wherever they went on the hotel grounds. She followed them when they took the bag with the dirty diapers to the dumpster, and then she skipped behind her until her nose pressed against their glass door. She must have known she wasn't supposed to come in, and she hadn't been invited, but she came terribly close. "We're in four," Cameron announced. "Right there." Pointing. "Okay, I guess. I'll see you later." When she backed away, her eyes were funny again, that same look, darting around to see if anybody was watching.

Shouldn't somebody be watching?

Jill remembered a time when she was a graduate teaching assistant at the University of Alabama, hanging out with boys, the kind of boys a good feminist wouldn't hang out with on a normal day—body-ogling, PBR-swigging boys who were fun to play pool with because they were smart and funny and could quote poetry even when they were many, many sheets to the wind. These boys were graduate teaching assistants just like her, and one day, an out-of-a-magazine co-ed from her English 101 class came into her office weeping about her life, pledging that she would do *anything* to make a C in the class. She was wearing a tank top over another tank top, both Lycra, no bra, and she put her breasts on the desk. Put them there. The act seemed unconscious—why would it be otherwise? force of habit?—but there they were, placed there, like a bottle of Coke or a literature anthology. On the desk. And she couldn't help but look at them, sitting there. She explained about the final paper and the revision process, but she was thinking: *Shit. My God. What if I wasn't me? What if I was one of those boys?*

Later, entering the red mouth of the Dali museum in St. Petersburg, Jill stopped to peer into the hole, and with one hand on the baby's stroller and the other on Dali's box, she could see that Cameron remembered everything exactly: the frame eyes, the fire nose, the couch mouth. "Don't you think that's pretty impressive, Mark?" she asked her husband. "She's only six."

"Not really," her husband said. "That's what you remember. You remember what's at the beginning and what's at the end."

She put her own eyes back up to the box and forced her mind to turn: a face, a living room, a face, a living room. The baby tossed her Dali finger puppet onto the floor and Jill took this as a signal to keep moving.

When they pulled into the hotel parking lot, she waved when she saw Cameron in the back seat of a white rental car. Cameron looked down without waving back. Jill couldn't see the other mother's eyes beneath her dark sunglasses, but she could tell she was looking right at her. The other mother's mouth was a straight line, a couch—no cushions. More of a bench, really.

In the morning, Cameron was not by the pool. The family had checked out.

Jill was disappointed. She had wanted to thank Cameron for recommending the museum. She wanted to tell her they'd touched the red fur, and everything in the box was just as Cameron had said it would be, she'd remembered exactly: a face, a living room, a face . . . and still, she had imagined saying to Cameron, there's no place to relax, is there? No place to sit, not without messing up the face. *What's that blot on the mouth? A bad tooth? A canker? Oh. No. It's Dad, sitting on the couch.* Jill had thought maybe this would make Cameron laugh. Such a serious little girl—she had wanted to make her laugh.

Outside the glass doors, the man worked on his boat, sanding down the bowsprit. He whistled while he worked. The day was so perfect, the sun on the water, it made her eyes hurt. Under the rippling surface, Jill imagined Cameron's shells, everything becoming sand.

She wiped the applesauce from the baby's face with a wet cloth and walked to the open door of the bedroom. She could see her husband lying spread-eagle on the floral bedspread. The straw fan on the wall was a kind of sombrero, the open fingers on each of his hands a fringe of flirty lashes, eyeball palms, head and torso nose, legs forming those lines that trace from our noses to the edges of our lips—what are those lines *called?* . . . but no mouth. She imagined curling herself onto the bottom of the bed to finish the picture. She could reach up and around her husband's feet, touch her fingers and toes to bold hibiscus cheeks on the horrible bedspread, and become a grinning mouth. Maybe she could grab the baby from her chair and plunk her, round and perfect, on the bottom corner. She could be a mole. A beauty mark!

Yes, she thought, scooping up the baby. That's what you remember. You remember what's at the beginning and what's at the end. Even if nobody was there to see her, she would be the smile.

The Right Tap

Lara Lillibridge

Hippocampus, 2016

I had forgotten how warm the water is straight out of the faucet in Key West. Open the cold tap, and you'll get water warm enough to bathe in. The water comes down a pipe one hundred and sixty miles from Miami, solar warm under the hot sun, saturated with dissolved makeup they used to say, or pipe rust or medication probably. I drank it anyway and didn't mind at all.

Cold hurts my soul. Winter always left me immobile-frozen to the sidewalk, eyebrows stinging needles, cold ache in my bones, fingers and toes blanched pale yellow. When it's cold, people cut you off in traffic and they don't have enough energy left to say hello to strangers, because all their molecules are busy keeping their body warm. It's not their fault. We are all ice frozen. Our insides need to thaw to let the goodness out.

But not here. Here the tap water greets you with warmth as you brush your teeth. Here is where I came when I walked out of my life, got in the car and drove until the road ended. Driving is healing: singing Gloria Gaynor to drown out the cat crying in the backseat, eating soggy egg sandwiches on hamburger buns you bought at Wal-Mart along with some Hanes Her Way because you left everything back in New York, except your pets and rollerblades. Driving to beat blizzards and driving through snow as far south as the Carolinas. It was a hard winter that year you escaped, a hard life you had to lead.

Sometimes crazy is a decision. Sometimes you are on the brink of it and can fall off either way. And if you straddle the limbo, life will choose your descent for you. Sometimes you flirt with crazy and let it flow in waves over your feet, beach-style, and a rip tide carries you out farther than you intended. And crazy is contagious. Sometimes when crazy is winning in your household you have to run away before it jumps on your back and digs its claws into your flesh. Sometimes you don't run soon enough, and you'll carry those scars for a while, but they will fade. Trust me, the mahogany lines turn pink, then silver, and in years to come you'll look down and be surprised that you can still see them, and that they aren't darker.

One day I drove and drove a stick-shift car, no cruise control, for four days. My dog, cat, stepmother riding along, radio blaring "I Will Survive." I drove through fear. It ebbed like the snow as I got farther south. His angry bald head—open mouth always yelling, shooting BB guns at the dogs, and a handgun in the backyard. Road rage, anger management, and too many prescription drugs—it all receded in my wake until I couldn't picture it clearly anymore. A good road trip will do that for you. I didn't have to be the sacrificial lamb to the promise I gave in church to stay until death did we part, which seemed to be just over the horizon. Mine anyway. I got in the old car, borrowed from my mother, the same model as the first one I ever drove, and the light-blue interior, worn-out seats, rusted doors, windup windows helped rewind me to who I had once been. I owned that car when I met him. It seemed fitting that in spite of all the new cars that came after, I left in the same model I came in with. I got in that car with my rollerblades and my favorite cat and one huge Rottweiler and five thousand dollars hidden in the trunk—my security, emptied from the bank right before it closed. I left him most of the money from the house fire insurance check, only taking enough to escape and pay the bills that were in my name. The road unraveled the ribbons of who I used to be until they fluttered free behind the moving car. The spool unwound until it was empty and I was ready to be wound in something new, wrapped up with who I yearned to be.

I pulled up in the driveway ten miles from the end of the road and the sky was filled with thoughts and stars. The air warm on my skin. All of my skin and hair was warm, even my toes and fingertips. And the cold-water faucet sent me more warm water.

I got a job, got a house, got friends, moved again and again and again and through all of it I was glad. I worked in gift shops with no air-conditioning into the dark of tourist winter and I was never too hot. I did not crave winter or seasons or tulips as much as I craved night-blooming jasmine and bougainvillea and lizards running from my feet on the hot sidewalk like mice. The things that I craved I was given here over and over, and other things I did not know I needed, like a church I didn't believe in but loved to attend, and bingo at a gay bar, and drag queens with sparkly pink lips. A gay roommate who chose my shoes and borrowed my clothes and taught me to watch *The Golden Girls* in bed after work, sometimes with wine even though he was underage, but just barely.

I got a boyfriend, then another husband I thought I wanted, and said I'd move north even though I had given away all my winter clothes because I had sworn that I was not going back, never. I was not crazy-mad in love with him, but he glowed with a halo that was probably just his red hair in the streetlight, but it was easy to mistake it for destiny. We never fought, and he was looking ahead in the same direction I was, and I knew I couldn't trust my heart to make good choices and I knew where crazy love got me before, so I knew I was better off without it.

We married in secret and this seemed to be the right path, so I quit my job, quit my life, quit my island, and packed the trunk with a thousand tiny bags and brought that same cat back off the island with me. The dog had been buried two years before. We got in my little red car, and I took down my sparkling drag queen fish that hung off my rearview mirror, because he said I had to. If it had to be done I would bury my own, not leave him to do it for me.

It turned out that looking in the same direction wasn't enough to base a life on, and I found in the end I could not live without that fish hanging from my rearview mirror. Five years later I hung it in my car once again, though the two-door red coupe was now a gold minivan filled with children's car seats, and this time I drove across town, not across the country.

I had my talisman fish but I couldn't go back south. Sometimes things can't be undone and this was one of them. And I stayed north where water flows cold from the cold tap, and snow falls from gray clouds on gray sidewalks.

But not always. There is summer and beaches and sunshine, and you forget that it isn't always like this until September slaps your face with hard cold reality and you can't drag summer out even one more day, though you beg and plead with the sky. And you say this year it won't be so bad in winter and by and by it is not that bad anymore in winter.

Then one day you come back south for two moons and a day. You don't remember streets or people's names, and you're a tourist not a local in what once felt like your hometown. And you realize you've lived north thirty-seven years and south only three, so why do you hang on to it as the place you were meant to live, when you were just a flash in the island's pan of revolving residents fried in oil served with a plantain? You turn on the cold tap, and warm water floods your hands, and then it all comes back how the island loved you and always gave you what you needed. And the faucet is shaped like Aladdin's lamp—unexpectedly bulbous—but it is granting you this wish, a promise that you can return. A promise that the warm Key West water that came all the way down the pipe from Miami will be waiting for your hands.

Hurricane

Karen Salyer McElmurray

River Teeth, 2012

Late summer, 2004. Later on, years and then months and finally weeks will converge in my memory as I try to recapture the exact color of my son's hair in the Florida sunlight, the exact tenor of his voice as we walked by the sea or as we talked by a window at breakfast.

What I remember.

Warm sand and tide. Shell fragments and thin silver fish touching my bare feet. My open hands up into the wind. Air smelling like electricity. A storm is moving inland. Somewhere back on shore, my son is photographing this moment. Take the camera, his mother said as we headed toward the beach.

I will rescript these moments with Andrew. I will make sentences and scenes and chapters out of my time with this son I do not really know.

Spring, 2004. Betty phoned me. She'd written me already, e-mails, then a note on her signature stationary. *BCC*. I hadn't answered yet, uncertain of how the vacation she proposed would be.

"It's a time-share," she said. Her voice is kind, its long Southern vowels breaking over me like oils and amber. I think of her like that, like something holy, like fragrances bathing the feet of travelers.

"Would there be room for John, too?" I asked.

Her time-share is in Siesta Key, on the west coast of Florida, on a stretch of white sand beach where she tells me there are the best shells she's ever found. She hikes each morning there, five miles and more. As I held the phone next to me and considered, I thought of her deep brown legs, the variations of tan and dark from her years in the sun.

"You and John will have to share the room with me and Aunt Rose," she said. "Jennie and Andrew will have the other room. The one downstairs."

How good this time would be, she said. Andrew would be comfortable, let down his guard, have time to relax. "Say you'll come. You and John."

And so we found us, my new husband, John, and me, driving through South Georgia and on into the bright, white sands of Florida. We stopped one night in Cedar Key, a resort town full of children with scooters and ice cream cones where we wandered along a concrete embankment next to the bay.

"What will it be like," I asked John. "Being there with all of them?"

There would be an Aunt. Betty, Andrew. His girlfriend, Jennie. I don't do well at holiday, even with my own sparse family, back in Kentucky. The urge to hide was overwhelming.

John, who has suffered the ups and downs and nothingness of my relationship with my son since it began with our reunion in 2002, sighed and pointed at the pelicans on buoys out in the water.

He wanted me to be present. To not make predictions about the future or about the shortcomings of what I had wanted. A miracle. An earth-transforming connection with the son I surrendered for adoption when I was 16. What I can have, John often says, is what all parents have. A share of time with a person who happens to be your child, but is more essentially on their own in this world, with their own ability to choose.

Below the concrete embankment, the waters of Cedar Key are mildly yellow, mildly listless in the hot August afternoon sun. I took the camera from John, turned it in the direction of shops and tourists with pink shoes and fruit drinks. Siesta Key, I told myself, would be a wilderness, an expanse of ocean and empty shores.

I have read the books on adoption and reunions. I know the stories. Female adoptees more likely to seek reunion with birth families in their 20s. Male adoptees more likely to seek such reunions in mid- to late 30s. Adoption reunions can be successful, but they can also be difficult in the best of worlds and impossible in many situations. After all the years apart, some mothers and children simply want nothing at all to do with the past. The past unearths forgotten deeds, better-left-behind actions. And sometimes, reunions unearth people too reminiscent of lives you could have led and can now never have or would definitely never want. And who knows, I've heard Betty, that most loving of mothers, say. In some cases, who knows what you could find?

On our first full day at Siesta Key, Andrew and the girlfriend, Jennie, had not yet arrived. That first evening was a travel reality show with Aunt Rose, then a sumptuous feast, the snacks of cheese and fruits and breads and sweets that Betty has purchased for our three-day vacation. Betty, Rose, and I slept in the bedroom, while John, shy and a gentleman, slept on the vinyl couch in the large front room. The morning we spent lounging by the pool at what is not, after all, a retreat with pristine, empty beaches and expanses of nothing but light and sand. Siesta Key was a popular spot for retirees and time-shares abounded. I had envisioned seafood and bait shops on a wharf somewhere, but hotels and fancy restaurants lined the busy streets. As I walked the beach that morning, I found myself dreaming of some unspecified, very long table in a room with windows open to fresh sea air. At that table, some family I've never seen, holding hands while a blessing was said.

Midafternoon, we set out, Betty and John and I, to pick up Andrew and Jennie at the Tampa airport, while Aunt Rose stayed behind to snooze in front of the TV. Betty and I were both nervous, a nervousness I played out by letting down the power window in the front seat too often, then letting it up again, so that Betty turned the AC up and down, trying to accommodate my fidgeting. Her own nervousness focused on bridges.

"I always hold my breath halfway over," she said as we headed across one of the arching passageways from one Tampa body of water to next. The bridges were sleek trails against the skyline.

"John's like that, too," I said over my shoulder. John was in the back seat, staring out at the bay. "Heights. Water."

Betty kept talking about the famous bridges she'd visited and hadn't, quite, been able to enjoy. San Francisco. Brooklyn. Even the bridge between Indiana and Kentucky, our mutual home state.

Andrew, she said, used to lay his child-hands against the car windows as they drove that bridge, the link between states. She always felt her heart fluttering, but Andrew. It was like, she said, he was framing the two worlds, in-car and out, with his two baby thumbs and his flat palms. She often refers, I have noted, to Andrew in this past tense, as small, a younger, less formed version of whoever it is he now has become. I fidgeted with the power window again, wondering what version of Andrew, which silhouette, would walk through the airport to greet us.

Over time, since our wintertime reunion in 2002, Andrew and I have seen each other only a handful of times. He lives in Arizona, I live in Georgia. Our rare meetings, I tend to see via images. I see my own hands held out and full of some dry, husky seeds that scatter and find no place to settle. I see my hands next to his hands, that first night we met, how we both clutched our wine glasses as if they were chalices, life-lines to keep us safe from each other. I was a writer-in-residence, then, at a small liberal arts university in the South. He was a graduate student in archaeology at a large state school in Arizona. We met because his girlfriend, Jennie, picked up my trail on the Internet, found photos of me, read portions of my memoir, the story of my relinquishment of a child to a state-supported adoption in Kentucky in 1973. We looked so much alike, Jennie wrote me, I just knew. And Andrew, she said, had long wanted to meet his birth mother. This too, is only a partial truth. Meeting. Eight years later, I still do not really know what Andrew thought of our meeting. When I think of that word, of my meeting with my son, I see lines on a map running parallel along an uneven coastline. These routes we might take skitter and halt, diverge, collide, move forward again. All of that, I think, will be clear now that we have met again, ocean-side, in this beautiful land of sun and horizons.

It's Jennie I saw first at the airport, a red-haired, Rubenesque young woman who walked past me in the lobby.

"Karen? I almost didn't recognize you," she said as she did an abrupt about-face.

We greeted each other with one of those two-cheek, in-the-air kisses. Jennie wasn't happy with me, these days, since my just-out book included photographs of her she found less than attractive. She was impeccable now, her full hair cut in layers since I saw her last. She pursed her lip, a speculative expression I recognized, as Andrew made his appearance behind me. We, too, greeted each other with loose-armed hugs, a kind of static electricity ebbing and waning between our bodies. If he's like me, I thought, he's been charged all day with waiting and not knowing exactly how to behave.

Later, too, after Betty had shown us all the room downstairs from the time-share, a small cubby kind of hole with a pull-down bed and a kitchen table and windows high on the walls, we sat awkwardly for awhile. I found myself checking the counters and the top of the fridge to see if Betty might have left us wine or snacks or other likely diversions. We had an hour left until our dinner reservations at a place that served an interesting mix of sushi and Italian.

As we talked, Andrew was fiddling with a Blackberry, checking in on the weather. Talking. That wasn't what we were really doing. We were all saying things, John, Jennie, Andrew, myself. We were sending out questions and statements and they crossed and uncrossed until I was reminded of those potholders children make with loops of cloth on metal frames. How was the flight? I asked. Or how was school, how was the weather in Arizona, how was the new apartment they just got? I thought about how often Andrew said yes, that one word, and how the word shaped itself in the air, a word with a question mark at the end like a tentative, cupped hand.

This is the kind of conversation families have, John has told me and he describes talking with his own children, a girl and boy who also call when they can, communicate what they want. Still, in this conversation, I was already attuned to each nuance, each tone of voice or raised eyebrow. I was looking for signs. Passageways. Anything to lead me inside the dark cave that is the son I do not know.

"Weather reports," Andrew said when I asked what he was looking for on the Blackberry.

Jennie leaned in and looked at the screen. "What are they saying now?"

"Storm warnings from the coast."

"It's storm season," John offered. He used to live in Florida.

"Yes," Andrew said.

All the while we were chatting about weather and airlines and layovers, about Andrew's previous visits to this time-share, and about the relative comfortableness of the pull-down from the wall bed the two of them will inhabit that night, I was studying this young man across the table from me. My son. Every time I'd seen him, he'd been newly disguised, his hair long, short, his sideburns profuse or absent. Sometimes he looked like Elvis to me, sometimes like some hippy I used to know, and sometimes like a younger, male version of myself.

Right away the next morning, we could all tell a storm was brewing. I could smell the storm in the trails of gourmet steam from the coffee Betty had brewed by the time we convened for a late breakfast, could taste the storm in air that drifted in from over the swimming pool behind the time share. Betty announced that she, too, had seen some weather reports, possible hurricane warnings, a system moving in from far out in the Atlantic. Nothing to worry about. She passed around toasted French bread wedges and fresh jam from the Siesta Key Farmer's Market.

What I felt like at this breakfast was a performing seal. I chattered and described—my life, my work, the town where I now lived, but Andrew had next to nothing to say. He was cutting his bread wedges into perfect, smaller bits, and carefully bedecking each portion with what I will later remember as scalding-hot foods. Chili slices. Pepper Jack.

"Andrew tolerates anything," Jennie said cheerfully. "Supper for breakfast."

"I'm like that." I joined in to the descriptions of cold, leftover pizza, hardened baked potatoes, halves of sandwiches on plates from the night before.

Andrew piled on torn leaves of lettuce and a dollop, on each bread slice, of wasabi. He studied me, head cocked to one side.

Before I knew it, other stories about what I am like fell from my lips. My propensity for vivid dreams. My love of books that I lose myself in over days and days, particularly on summer afternoons with white wine in tall, blue glasses. I wanted Andrew to meet my eyes, address me directly, but he didn't. I talked out of turn, my voice nervous, my stories on the edge of nonsensical. A laugh too much like my own mother's fell from my lips. It was only ten o'clock in the morning.

"Do you want to take a walk with me," I asked Andrew at last. "Talk?"

A silence fell on the group and Andrew rearranged his toasted bits, made a semi-circle facing himself. Everyone waited, breath held.

"Yes," he said at last, that open-ended statement again, a statement and a question and some other, undefined quality. I've been told by employers and interviewers and lovers, all, that I answer the things I'm uncomfortable with in just the same way.

Meanwhile, Betty was taking up the slack, reminding us of the long day ahead of us. Plans for lunch, shell walks on the beach, a swim before drinks. Dinner reservations. Food piled up in front of us all, plates of it, planned portions of it. I inched toward the door and Betty followed me. She showed me her shell collection from the recent days past, shells gleaming with oil to make their colors shine. I opened the door, looked back, but Andrew hadn't followed me yet. Through the open door, wind from the parking lot, stirring the flat leaves of a live oak. The storm, Betty said, couldn't amount to much.

It's in all the papers from that time, the hurricane. *Charley*. Second major hurricane of the 2004 Atlantic hurricane season. *At its peak of intensity of 150 mph, Hurricane Charley struck the northern tip of Captiva Island and the southern tip of North Captiva Island, causing severe damage in both areas.* Landfall near Port Charlotte. North by northeast along the Peace River corridor. Devastation in Punta Gorda, Cleveland, Fort Ogden, Nocatee, Arcadia, Zolfo Springs, Wauchula. Masses of large trees, power poles, power lines, transformers, debris filling the streets. Damage in the state, up to $13 billion.

And yet in my memory, 2004 fades into 2006. 2001 becomes 2010. *Now. Then. Now.* Fine rain and wind bear down in this memory. Floodgates open and bridges sway. The sky is a vortex, its center opening in all the years ahead. The only still point I can find is the center of me.

Womb. The word is like bats and caves, like the wrinkled faces of the just born. If I can imagine that place, I think I can make the world be still. Black clouds cross the sun.

By midmorning on the day after we've all convened at the beach, the news was full of warnings. *Evacuate. Storm moves inland. Landfall in southwestern Florida.* The strongest hurricane to hit the United States since Hurricane Andrew struck Florida 12 years before, in 1992.

We raced from time-share to cars, loading our stuff. Up stairs. Down, arms laden with all the things we'd need for our chosen spot, somewhat north, dead-center inland. We'd sat at breakfast and John, the practical one, had spread out maps and road atlases, while Betty, his co-pilot, had located the names of hotels in her Triple A guides. We were soon marked for Lakeland, Florida, Hampton Inn, near enough to the Interstate for a quick escape farther north, if we needed it, and near enough south to Siesta Key, should the storm pass over and leave us our two days of vacation ahead. We left behind the majority—the fridge still well-stocked, shells still strewn across the end tables and the counters. We stuffed bags with nightgowns and shoes, with cell phones and books. John and I packed all we'd brought since, hurricane or not, we'd head on back to Georgia after the storm. Backtracking made no sense.

By one o'clock we'd settled again, bags in rooms, toothbrushes on the vanities, and we were sitting with a dozen other people in the motel lobby, glued to the television set, watching the storm nudge Category Three, head for Category Four. Hurricane Charley. A small, fast-moving storm, its high winds already tearing down power utilities, smashing cars, lifting huge trees up by their roots. In the end, Hurricane Charley will cause 10 deaths and will be the second-costliest hurricane in U.S. history. For the next two days, we'll watch newscasters in their waders and raincoats. We'll watch reporters at their desks, checking in with cities and contacts until the lines can't be reached. They're almost like family, Jennie said, as she poured a cup of instant coffee and settled next to me. The skies, heavy and low, slanted rain against the motel windows.

When I was little, I wanted time out of time. I wanted strolls in parks with my mother and father and me, hand in hand. I wanted an island somewhere, a paradise of love. Or this. I wanted what I could not have. A happy family, two and one and three. I was not that happy child, nor were my parents the givers of happiness. They did not know how to draw empty squares on a page titled "home" and fill up the squares with tables and chairs and roasted chickens on Wedgewood plates. They missed the script, somewhere back in their own childhoods. I was their issue and hence-forward on my own. I wandered the earth after that, seeking to fill in my own blank spaces. My son is one of these. A blank line on a form with a name written in. I gave him away at birth. I signed the papers. And now, with a storm unfolding over us, I am inviting him back in.

All night, rain. Rain hard enough to keep me awake as sheets flooded against the thick glass of the Hampton Inn bedroom windows. John was snoring and the rain was nonstop and so I got up early, headed down to the free breakfast bar. I was filling my plate with sausage links and scrambled egg patties when I saw Andrew. Andrew heading out of the elevators on the opposite end of the lobby. He had a book under his arm and he stood with it near the front desk awhile, thumbing through the pages, glancing up now and then to scan the still fairly empty lobby. He was, I thought, one of the most beautiful men I'd ever seen. I memorized his longish light-brown hair tied back with a rubber band, his loose gray shorts, a striped cotton shirt with a tear in the sleeve.

He saw me in a bit and he jumped. I'd noticed him doing that over the two days of this vacation. He jumped and twitched when he saw me watch-ing him, a brief spasmodic sort of nervous energy that made me wonder about what he thought of what he knew about me. Drug days. My preg-nancy as an on-the-run teenager, malnourished days of nurturing him in-side a 15-year-old body. He twitched now as he walked up, grabbed a plate and began to fill it with fruit and biscuits.

"What are you reading?" I asked. I nodded at the book tucked under his arm.

"History," he mumbled. He studied the array of jams and margarine cubes.

"I loved history." I began to list the ways. Russian history. Medieval his-tory. Appalachian history.

Midway through my recitation, he interrupted me, laid down his book. "It's about Neo-Nazis," he said.

He began again to stack things on the already burgeoning plate. Bacon slices. Untoasted English muffins. He nodded at the tray. "For Jennie."

"Well," he said. "See you in a bit."

"Well," I said.

Rain pelted harder and I heard it again as the lobby door swung open. I wondered if hurricanes make thunder.

Make a list on a page you keep just for yourself, a friend tells me. List all of the things you think you'd want in this relationship with your son. Hand holding down sunny lanes in a forest, maybe? Sea shells by the seashore. Family meals at picnic tables in state parks? I do want the scripts in my head, I admit it. The perfect times I could have had and surrendered once and for all. Or maybe what I want is this: a miracle. I wrote a book about the surrender of my child and that book summoned him from the past and made him part of my present. Wasn't that the miracle? It doesn't seem this is the case. My son sits in my presence like a stone, a statue-boy from my dreams. I'm waiting for him to speak. To love me from this moment on and from the beginning, completely and forever.

What Betty did not know, when she booked us all for Hampton Inn until the hurricane moves past, is that friends of hers were there too. Last night she introduced John and myself to them—mother and daughter, a couple I will call Mrs. Hyatt and Nora. Mrs. Hyatt, a plump woman with plump ankles and white leather shoes, is in Betty's book discussion group back in Kentucky. Nora, the daughter, is visiting from some city on the west coast and, just by chance, we'd all ended up evacuated together during one of the storms of the century. Last night, Betty'd shown Andrew off to the Hyatts, her arm draped around Andrew's waist, her strong, proud-mother laugh mixing with theirs as they all made acquaintance.

I was jealous of the Hyatts and, since we got to the Hampton Inn, jealous of Betty. Jealous of her thin, be-ringed hand, how it lay protectively on Andrew's knee as we watched The Weather Family tracking the path of the hurricane. My jealousy mixed bitterly with my jam and toast as I sat by myself at a table in the lobby, then looked up to find Nora Hyatt poised near me, plate in hand.

"Feel like company?" she asked.

I was reading, but I laid the book aside, opened on its spine, and studied Nora, her shorts with pleats ironed in. She was studying me, too.

We sipped our coffee and talked books. The latest best sellers. The discussion group's choice of Kentucky women writers for their fall line-up.

"I've read your memoir," she said at last. She set her plate down, a meager arrangement of fruit and healthy toast and a spoon of eggs that made my own plate, its waffle and eggs and links and everything else, seem gargantuan.

"Thank you," I said.

"It's so moving." She forked up some eggs, patted them onto a wedge of wheat toast. I nodded.

"But isn't it hard," she said and paused. She looked at me.

"Yes," I began, prepared to talk about the reunion she must know about. Her mother's book group and Betty's. They've discussed the memoir.

"Having all that love." She sighed and looked down.

"Love," I echoed, and again I was ready to hold forth, talk about what it feels like to imagine love, then to see it walk in the door, sit in the room with me, evacuate with me on a Florida vacation.

"All that love," she continued. "For someone who doesn't want it."

The dream was this. We'd convene by the sea and heal in its warm waters. Play and laugh and unwind. But secretly, my wish was for a baptism, a renewal. Ocean water sprinkled on the heads of the redeemed. And yet we have seen the ocean only once. I stood in the ocean on the morning the hurricane began to move north and I raised my hands like a dancer. Watch me, I was thinking, and I pirouetted and turned for my son as if I was content. Happy, even. What did he see when he looked out toward the horizon? His mother? I don't think so. How young I must seem to him, this woman not quite 16 years his senior. How could that woman dipping and turning in the waves be a mother? Why, look at her in her pretty bathing suit, her hair tied back and her slim hands waving. His mother. She's back there, arranging cookies on a tray, making all the world just right. That mother, this mother. Women dance in his head and, really, he wants none of them at all. He snaps a photograph, just as he has been told.

On our last night in Florida, the hurricane slid farther north, then headed east unexpectedly, missed Tampa. Made its way out to the coast again and disappeared over the horizon, back to the land of other brewing storms. In the night I dreamed this storm, that it climbed up out of a swimming pool outside the hotel, a storm like a finned god with big hands. Now, I got up while the hotel was still mostly dark. I eased the door shut, left John deeply asleep, padded down the carpeted hall.

In the lobby, they'd already started filling up the breakfast trays, heaping up the big plate of free cookies at the registration desk. I paused, broke off the edge of a cookie, stood for awhile with chocolate melting on my tongue. The morning was quiet, gentler sheets of rain slanted earthward now. I thought about how it could be. Heading back upstairs, stuffing all my things into a bag or two, leaving all of it behind. John and I could make like cowboys, movie stars riding into the sunrise, escaping before the day really begins. I could unmother me, leave my history behind forever.

Or I could head out the lobby doors. Could walk far enough from the hotel that no one could see me at all from a window or a bedroom. I could stand out there, behind a parked car or around the corner of the building, or the one next door. I could turn my face up to the rain and wait, the waters of forgetting at last washing me clean, absolving me of everything. Like that, there would be no son, no mother, no womb that roils like the sea, remembering its own history. I could do this.

I stood by these wide doors and watched them, a cleaning crew just coming in. They sprayed and moved their slow white cloths against fingerprints and dust. The doors opened, shut. A mist of rain swept against my face.

Even You, Miami

Susannah Rodríguez Drissi

Saw Palm, 2016

When I was nine years old, we climbed into my uncle's 1958 green Ford and, just like that, we went away. We left behind very little or everything. I didn't turn to look back once at the vanishing faces, the schools, the park, the church, the stray dogs, and that damn lagoon in Bauta bubbling pestilence and rancor in the distance. The last nine years already brittle against the car window's glass, as we drove to the airport. I didn't squint toward the skyline to the hot, silent roofs of our small town. Our old bodies like holograms fading in small bursts of light on the road behind us, yielding our spaces to newcomers. I didn't cry. My younger sister did that, gripping my grandmother's thigh. Small fingers wrestling my mother's hands for their right to stay put right where we were. Instead, I dug clean nails on bare legs. Eyes pinned to the road ahead. Ears tuned to pebbles crushing under tires. Chin parallel to the car's window frame. Muscles, ligaments, tendons, and bones turned to stone—twitching from the tension, they would never recover. All the while, holding my breath.

For twenty-five years I'd waited for the memory of that hot, tongue-tied, random night to wane. Waited for the town to fade into sun-bleached bare roadways I'd no longer wish to turn to. Waited for the phantom pain to dissipate. It wasn't Cuba I longed for. It was those first nine years of childhood. Sacred and burdened by too much knowing. Knowing then, as I know now that leaving the island was an irreversible step. It would all speed up from that point forward. We'd be farther and farther away from small, wrinkled hands picking insects out of rice on wooden tables. From small feet sidestepping slivers of bottle-green glass and *uvas caletas*. Further away from lime-green frogs on rainy days. From fireflies banging heads against glass jars. From neighbors shouting and raging, spitting on blinds closed shut. From raucous mobs scratching at pupils peering through the window. And further still from ourselves. We, too, would never—we have never recovered.

A place becomes us and we become that place. Our bodies move this or that way to adjust to the particulars of the space, to the needs and burdens of the place we inhabit. At nine years old, my hands swatted mosquitoes feasting on my neck, tied knots on sweat-drenched ponytails, folded flags the right way, dug impatient fingers into hot sand for iridescent shells. Eyes squinting at the sun—I was just the right size for my age. Adolescence and California would wreak havoc on my body. I was often too tall or too short, depending on where I was and with whom. Too skinny or too fat. Too fair or reproachably tan. My eyebrows too bushy or just like Brooke Shields's. No noticeable gap—never—between my thighs. My hands always flailing, saying way too much when my tongue got caught between my teeth. Except for the unwavering constant of Southern California's reasonable, temperate climate, all was misapplied, misshapen, and out of place. Nothing to do but return.

So I did—many times, in fact. I returned on my first trip to New Orleans. Palm trees, Persian blinds, above-ground cemeteries, and jazz. But too much English. Then, there was Paris clad in cobblestones, cabarets, Cubans rushing to and fro out of Spanish bars near La Bastille, and the charred sweetness of fried plantains in Barbès. But most spoke French. In any case, the Mississippi and the Seine muscled the ruse into the realm of comparable bodies of water. Finally, after much travel, a port city: Alger la Blanche. I'd travel all the way to North Africa to return. It was then hard to tell the difference between our palm trees and theirs, between their jousting and ours, between their music and ours. But there was one fundamental difference: walking down the street, I took up too much space. Once again, my hands moved in inappropriate ways. Far, too far from my body. I looked too much into the eyes of store clerks and passersby. There were no black beans or rice and, certainly, no fried plantains. And I was not Cuban, but American. Only in Cuba, I thought, could I be Cuban. So, after twenty-five years, I went back.

The past would finally give up its ghost and I cried big, fat tears where none had been possible decades before. Muscles yielding to the heat, my body supple again. But I might as well have been in New Orleans or Paris or Algiers—the fit wasn't quite right. Upon returning to my childhood home, I discovered that it had been divided in two. A wall split the old house into two equitable, livable domains. I was way too big for either space. The ceiling was not high enough and to walk from the living room to the kitchen required only a few small steps. What for twenty-five years had seemed a distant palace, was now a small, sickly home, with falling slabs of paint and barely enough space to stretch out one's neck and grow. "What of the lagoon," I asked. "Oh," one of the new owners said, "dried up a long time ago." At least that, I thought. It had never seemed a lake.

One by one, I returned to those places that had meant something to me: my elementary school, the park, the corner market, the church and the bell tower, the local beach. Those spaces that had shaped my body in ways that had since then rendered fitting in anywhere else an uncomfortable and disheartening experience. Better fit for a contortionist than an exile. Cuba had proven to be as much a trick of the eye as any other country I'd sought to return to in its place. Then, one day, I found myself in Miami.

Miami, where everyone is more Cuban than Cubans in Cuba. Where mothers pin up time to hair rollers and *torniquetes*. Where the nauseating sweetness of Agua de Violeta mixes with the pungent, cool burn of Vicks VapoRub. Where names like Papito and Magaly somersault from salty tongues into the streets. Where Spanish muscles English out of the way and hands do what they do free from containment. Miami. Little Cuba. Little haven for bodies on the run. Cuba almost in the palm of one's hand, quivering. Moist and sticky like a newborn chick. I want to take you home. But even you, Miami, are not the right fit.

Familiar Shore

Jim Ross

Paper Tape Magazine, 2014

I am standing on the beach at North Captiva Island, Florida. It is 4:30 on a July afternoon and I'm gazing at the most beautiful natural sight I've ever seen. The sun shines onto the sea, making the Gulf of Mexico look like a giant sheet of wavy green velvet on which a million diamonds sparkle. Before me is a strip of white sand. Behind me is a dead tree, perched on the edge of a protected preserve overgrown with palms, sea oats, and salty scrub.

Like most Florida residents, I grew up someplace else. I was raised and educated near Chicago and came to Florida during college for reporting internships at the *St. Petersburg Times* and the *Miami Herald*. At age 21 I returned for a full-time job at the *Times*.

Florida is a top newspaper state, and I rode a tide of young journalism school graduates who stormed ashore to Do Great Things. The *Herald* was exposing Gary Hart. The *Times* was a writer's paper that nurtured future Pulitzer winners. Florida was the place to be. Leaving home was tough, but I wanted to make a splash.

The years passed and most of my contemporaries left for bigger professional waters: Washington, D.C., New York, the Midwest powers. The glory days faded. Florida newspapers still do excellent work but they struggle financially. My *Times* bureau closed in 2007 because of corporate cutbacks. I went to the *Ocala Star-Banner*.

Despite it all I remain in Florida. I am 46, and I have lived here more years (25) than anywhere else. Why? I have no extended family here. I don't have Disney season passes. I can't fish, can't hunt, can barely swim. Man has yet to invent a sunscreen strong enough to protect my fair skin. The middle-management, parental "life" that I lead—editing copy, chauffeuring kids, mowing the lawn—could be lived anywhere. Show a video account of my average day to a stranger and he won't know in which state the action is happening.

Defending Florida residency is no easier at the macro level. The land is famously crammed with condos, golf courses, and strip malls, and populated with grifters, confidence men, and rapacious developers. Hurricanes threaten and cockroaches terrorize. The writer Jeff Klinkenberg reminds us that in Manhattan we can get mugged, but only in Florida can we swim in a lake and get eaten alive by a dinosaur: an alligator.

My siblings ask why I don't move back home to Illinois, which they never left, and no easy answer comes to me. Inertia, perhaps. Resistance to discarding adult comforts like church, doctors, and schools. Reluctance to abandon a job that pays the bills. Are these reasons or default positions?

Then one Sunday I load my wife and three kids into the minivan and drive four hours from Ocala to southwest Florida. We ferry across the choppy water to North Captiva Island, which can't be reached by car. The hot sand singes my feet and the salty sea breeze brushes my face. I squint west into the horizon, hoping a dolphin will leap from beneath those sparkling diamonds.

And I realize: I am a bit exposed, unmoored, unsettled about my place. But that has an unexpected positive side. It leaves me open to these unguarded moments, these rushes of awe and pride for my adopted state—and for myself. I left home, built a life and raised a family in this crazy, intoxicating, magnetic place. I didn't stay on, or return to, familiar shore.

Not far from where I stand, spread on the beach like a tray of jewels, are countless seashells. They have exotic names like conch, whelk, and cockle. They are pearl white, chocolate brown, coral green. Some are ridged, some fluted, some smooth to the touch. Step on one and you'll be cut. Hold one in your hand and you'll see a unique, dignified beauty.

Some shells will be gone with the next tide or the one after that. Others will remain ashore until who knows when. There's no telling which fate awaits which shell. But the ones on higher ground, the ones least likely to drift back to sea, look perfectly placed. From a distance they are part of some random, motley design. Up close, they rest comfortably in the sand, as if they have somehow nestled into that one spot in the world where they were always meant to be.

Acknowledgments

Thanks to Sian Hunter, Ali Sundook, and the entire team at the University Press of Florida for making this book possible. Thanks to Lucy Bryan and my wife, Melanie, for expert editing, manuscript guidance, and support. Kate Hopper, Ana Maria Spagna, and Richard Gilbert helped identify work that would be a good fit. Bill McKeen helped inspire the idea for this book with his own volume, *Homegrown*, and was a valuable adviser throughout the process. Rob Bradshaw provided expert advice as the project got started.

Special thanks to Joe Mackall, Dan Lehman, Sarah Wells, and the entire *River Teeth* family. That is my essaying tribe, and I am proud to stand with them.

All of the essays in this anthology (except two) were previously published in literary journals and magazines. Special thanks to the authors and publications for granting reprint permissions. And thanks to the editors at those publications for helping bring these essays to life.

Finally, thanks again to Melanie and our kids, James, Anna, and Kate, for being patient with me as this project took shape. A man couldn't have a better family.

Contributors

Chantel Acevedo's novels include *Love and Ghost Letters*, which won the Latino International Book Award and was a finalist for the Connecticut Book of the Year; *Song of the Red Cloak*, a historical novel for young adults; *A Falling Star*, winner of the Doris Bakwin Award and the National Bronze Medal IPPY Award; and *The Distant Marvels*, a Carnegie Medal finalist and an Indie Next Pick. Her latest novel, *The Living Infinite*, is forthcoming. She is also the author of *En Otro Oz*, a chapbook of poems. Her short stories, essays, and poems have appeared in *Prairie Schooner*, *American Poetry Review*, *North American Review*, and *Ecotone*, among many others. She is currently associate professor of English at the University of Miami and advises *Sinking City*, the literary journal of the university's MFA program.

Jan Becker is from a small coal-mining town in Pennsylvania. She didn't stay there very long. She grew up in a Marine Corps family, on military bases all over the United States, and wandered the United States for many years before settling in South Florida. Becker's memoir, *The Sunshine Chronicles*, was published in 2016. Her work has appeared in *Jai-Alai Magazine*, *Colorado Review*, *Emerge*, *Brevity Poetry Review*, *Sliver of Stone*, and *Florida Book Review*. She is the winner of the 2015 AWP Intro Journals Award in Nonfiction.

Marion Starling Boyer's "Bingo Territory" was first published in the September 2016 issue of *River Teeth*. Her essays have also appeared in *Tishman Review*, *Paddler*, *American Whitewater*, *Canoe & Kayak*, and *Great Lakes Review*. Boyer has published three poetry collections: *The Clock of the Long Now* (2009), *Green* (2003), and *Composing the Rain*, which won the Grayson Books 2014 poetry chapbook competition. Boyer writes from Michigan, where the lake-effect snows encourage her to continue to escape to Florida for February.

Rick Bragg is an American journalist and writer known for nonfiction books, especially those about his family in Alabama. He won a Pulitzer Prize in 1996 recognizing his work at the *New York Times*. He is a regular contributor *to Southern Living Magazine* and *Garden & Gun*.

Jennifer S. Brown is a former Floridian grudgingly adapting to New England winters. Although she misses sunlight and stone crabs, she's developed a fondness for lobster rolls and snowshoeing. She has published fiction and creative nonfiction in *Cognoscenti, The Best Women's Travel Writing, Southeast Review*, and *Bellevue Literary Review*, among other places. Her novel *Modern Girls*, set in 1935 New York City, is about a mother and daughter who must face the consequences of unplanned and unwanted pregnancies. Find her at www.jennifersbrown.com.

Lucy Bryan grew up in Orlando, Florida, where she developed a fondness for reptiles, a fear of flying insects, and a taste for fresh fish. She now lives in the Shenandoah Valley and contents herself with gazing at mountains on the days she can't climb them. She teaches writing at James Madison University. Her essays and short stories have appeared in *Quarterly West, Nashville Review, Word Riot*, and *Superstition Review*, among others.

Linda Buckmaster has lived within a block of the Atlantic most of her life, growing up in "Space Coast" Florida during the 1950s and 1960s and being part of the back-to-the-land movement in midcoast Maine in the 1970s. Her poetry, essay, and fiction have appeared in more than thirty journals, and one of her pieces was listed as a Notable Essay in *Best American Essays 2013*. She has held residencies at Vermont Studios Center, Atlantic Center for the Arts, and Obras Foundation, among others. She blogs at lsbuck1.blogspot.com.

Jill Christman is the author of *Darkroom: A Family Exposure* (AWP Award Series in Creative Nonfiction winner); *Borrowed Babies: Apprenticing for Motherhood* (2014); and essays in magazines such as *Brevity, Fourth Genre, Iron Horse Literary Review, TriQuarterly, Oprah Magazine, River Teeth*, and *Brain, Child*. She serves on the board of the Association of Writers and Writing Programs (AWP) and teaches creative nonfiction writing in Ashland University's low-residency MFA program and at Ball State University in Muncie, Indiana. She was born in the now-defunct Miami Baby Hospital while her older brother watched Cookie the Crocodile swallow live chickens at the also obsolete Serpentarium. Visit her at www.jillchristman.com.

Susannah Rodríguez Drissi is a Cuban poet, writer, translator, and scholar. She is lecturer and visiting research fellow in comparative literature at UCLA. Her writing has appeared in *Saw Palm, Literal Magazine, Diario de Cuba (Madrid), SX Salon, Raising Mothers, Acentos Review*, and *Cuba Counterpoints*, among other journals. She is contributing and review editor at *Cuba Counterpoints*. She lives in Los Angeles with her husband and two daughters. Her first novel, tentatively titled "Until We're Fish," is under review at a literary press.

Sarah Fazeli, a native of Columbus, Ohio, spent the past fifteen years in Los Angeles working as an actor, yoga teacher, and writer. She has been published in xoJane.com and *Narratively* and has appeared on HuffPost Live to discuss a widely read essay. She recently moved back to Ohio with her dog, Sadie, who "works" as a therapy dog in hospice. She is in the final revisions of a memoir.

Corey Ginsberg's prose and poetry have most recently appeared in such publications as *Minnesota Review, PANK, cream city review, Subtropics, Los Angeles Review*, and *Nashville Review*. Corey currently lives in Miami and works as a freelance writer and editor.

Lauren Groff is the author of *The Monsters of Templeton*, short-listed for the Orange Prize for New Writers; *Delicate Edible Birds*; and *Arcadia*, a New York Times Notable Book, winner of the Medici Book Club Prize, and finalist for the L.A. Times Book Award. Her third novel, *Fates and Furies*, was a finalist for the National Book Award in Fiction, the National Book Critics Circle Award, and the Kirkus Award. It was a *New York Times* Notable Book and Bestseller, Amazon.com's #1 book of 2015, and appeared on more than two dozen best-of-2015 lists. Her work has appeared in journals including *The New Yorker, Atlantic Monthly, Harper's, Tin House, One Story*, and *Ploughshares*, and in the anthologies *100 Years of the Best American Short Stories; The Pushcart Prize: Best of the Small Presses; PEN/O. Henry Prize*

Stories; and four editions of the *Best American Short Stories*. She lives in Gainesville, Florida, with her husband and two sons.

Katelyn Keating serves as editor-in-chief of *Lunch Ticket,* where she formerly edited the Diana Woods Memorial Award and the nonfiction genre, and wrote essays as a staff blogger. She is a 2017 fellow of The LARB/USC Publishing Workshop. Hailing from New England, she lives in St. Augustine, Florida, with her family. Her essays and reviews have been published in *Lunch Ticket*, and she has work forthcoming in *Crab Orchard Review*. She is completing an essay collection and is at work on a novel.

Sandra Gail Lambert is the author of *A Certain Loneliness: A Memoir* (2018) and the novel *The River's Memory*. Her writing is often about the body and its relationship to the natural world and has been published in a variety of journals and anthologies including the *Southern Review* and *The Best Women's Travel Writing*. She is also a coeditor of the anthology *Older Queer Voices: The Intimacy of Survival*. She lives in Gainesville, Florida— a home base for trips to her beloved rivers and marshes. Her website is www.sandragaillambert.com.

Lara Lillibridge is the author of *Girlish: Growing Up in a Lesbian Home* (2017). In 2016 she won *Slippery Elm Literary Journal*'s prose contest, and the *American Literary Review*'s contest in nonfiction. She has had essays published in *Pure Slush Vol. 11*, *Vandalia*, and *Polychrome Ink*; and on the web at *Hippocampus, Crab Fat Magazine, Luna Luna, Huffington Post, Feminist Wire, Airplane Reading, Thirteen Ways to Tell a Story*, and *Weirderary Literature Magazine*.

Bill Maxwell first joined the *Tampa Bay Times* in 1994 as an editorial writer. He also wrote a twice-weekly column. In 2004, he left to teach journalism and establish a program at Stillman College in Alabama, but he returned to the board in August 2006. A native of Fort Lauderdale, Maxwell was reared in a migrant farming family. After a short time in college and the U.S. Marine Corps, he returned to school. During his college years, he worked as an urban organizer for the Southern Christian Leadership Conference and wrote for several civil rights publications. He first began teaching college English in 1973 at Kennedy-King College in Chicago and continued to teach for 18 years. Before joining the *Times*, Maxwell spent six years writing a weekly column for the *Gainesville Sun* and the *New York Times* syndicate. Before that, Maxwell was an investigative reporter for the *Fort Pierce Tribune*, focusing on labor and migrant farmworker affairs.

Karen Salyer McElmurray's *Surrendered Child: A Birth Mother's Journey*, was an AWP Award Winner for Creative Nonfiction. Her novels are *The Motel of the Stars*, Editor's Pick by *Oxford American*; and *Strange Birds in the Tree of Heaven*, winner of the Chaffin Award for Appalachian Writing. "Elixir" was a Notable Essay in *Best American Essays 2016*. With poet Adrian Blevins, she has coedited a collection of essays, *Walk till the Dogs Get Mean: Meditations on the Forbidden from Contemporary Appalachia*.

Deesha Philyaw is coauthor of *Co-Parenting 101: Helping Your Kids Thrive in Two Households after Divorce*, written in collaboration with her ex-husband. Her writing on parenting, race, gender, and culture has appeared in the *New York Times, Washington Post, Pittsburgh Post-Gazette, Full Grown People, Brevity, Dead Housekeeping, The Establishment, Catapult*, ESPN's *The Undefeated*, and elsewhere. Deesha's work includes a Notable Essay in *The Best American Essays 2016*. At the *Rumpus*, Deesha inaugurated and curates an interview column called "VISIBLE: Women Writers of Color."

Lisa Roney is the author of *Serious Daring: Creative Writing in Four Genres* (2015); *The Best Possible Bad Luck* (2014); and *Sweet Invisible Body* (1999/2000). Her short fiction, nonfiction, and poetry have appeared in *Harper's, Saw Palm, Inside Higher Ed, So to Speak, Sycamore Review*, and other publications. She is associate professor of English at the University of Central Florida and editor and director of the *Florida Review* and *Aquifer: The Florida Review Online*.

Jim Ross is managing editor and columnist at the *Ocala (FL) Star-Banner* and adjunct journalism instructor at the University of Florida. His journalism and essays have been published in the *Star-Banner, St. Petersburg Times, Gainesville Sun, Clockhouse Review, Little Patuxent Review* blog, *Foliate Oak Literary Magazine, Paper Tape Magazine, Morning News, Ray's Road Review*, and the *Eastern Iowa Review*. "This Is How I Post" was a Notable

Essay in *Best American Essays 2015*, and "Slow to Learn" was a Notable in *Best American Essays 2016*. He lives in Ocala with his wife and three kids.

Lia Skalkos grew up in the woods of New Hampshire and amid the cicadas of Athens, Greece. When she's not working as a software engineer in New York City, she's trying to find a way to get outdoors or writing from her home in Hoboken, New Jersey.

Credits

Made in the USA
Coppell, TX
11 August 2021